# ATLANTIS AND THE SEVEN STARS

# ATLANTIS AND THE SEVEN STARS

J. COUNTRYMAN

ST. MARTIN'S PRESS
NEW YORK

**Library of Congress Cataloging in Publication Data**
Countryman, Jack.
  Atlantis and the seven stars.
  Bibliography : p.
  Includes index.
  1. Interplanetary voyages.   2. Atlantis.
3.  Pleiades.   I.  Title.
CB156.C69      001.9′4      77–9182
ISBN  0–312–05946–9

# CONTENTS

# ACKNOWLEDGEMENTS

The author wishes to thank the following for permission to quote from copyright material: Ballantine Books, for extracts from *Lost Continents* by L. Sprague de Camp; Arthur C. Clarke, Scott Meredith Literary Agency Inc. and David Higham Associates Ltd, for an extract from *The Exploration of Space* by Arthur C. Clarke; R. S. Crocker Co. Inc., for extracts from *The Secret Teachings of All Ages* by Manly P. Hall; Faber and Faber, for an extract from *The Discovery of the Universe* by Gerard de Vaucouleurs; the Loeb Society and Heinemann Educational Books for extracts from Plato; Penguin Books, for extracts from the *Odyssey* by Homer; G. P. Putnam's Sons and Souvenir Press, for an extract from *Voyage to Atlantis* by James W. Mavor; Neville Spearman, for an extract from *Sons of the Sun* by Marcel Homet; Pelham Books Ltd, for an extract from *Did Spacemen Colonize the Earth?* by Robin Collyns; Dover Publications Inc., for an extract from *Star Names, their Lore and Meaning* by Richard Hinkley Allen.

Of the above I am particularly indebted to L. Sprague de Camp's *Lost Continents* for a number of the basic facts contained in Chapter Six, though my conclusions are quite different from those of Mr de Camp.

Many a night I saw the Pleiads,
rising thro' the mellow shade,
Glitter like a swarm of fire-flies
tangled in a silver braid.

Tennyson

# INTRODUCTION

## The Earth and the Pleiades in a Universe Pulsating with Life

OUR GALAXY, the Milky Way, a spiral structure, has a diameter of a hundred thousand light years. Only 400 light years from Earth by comparison, in this structure are our neighbours the Pleiades. It is within the depths of the Pleiades that one day may be found a large number of planets—worlds of infinite life, worlds void of life, worlds beginning life, perhaps even worlds identical to our present world. What may be regarded as pure fantasy by one planet may be the stark reality of another.

The Pleiades are a young cluster but astronomers theorize that it is still possible for high-level civilizations to evolve there because of the still unknown factors that could cause evolution in the universe. Perhaps in this cluster we have sister planets that are historically, anthropologically, and culturally connected to Earth. One of these planets may be the birth place of Poseidon who was instrumental in bringing a high form of civilization to Earth. Astronomers theorize a million advanced planets in our galaxy alone and communication between them would be inevitable.

Our glittering galaxy transcends all comprehension. Only the glaze of this celestial wonder is reflected in its flickering suns and synchronized pulsars, leaving untold mysteries for the surface impressions of our telescopes. Plato likened men to prisoners in a cave, watching shadows on the opposite wall cast by a fire. We earthmen dwelling on our tiny planet around an insignificant sun sited in obscurity amidst more galaxies than there are grains

9

of sand on every beach in the world, can have little conception of the realities of the cosmos.

The vast uncharted depths of the universe could even contain demigods, super-gods, giants and fabulous civilizations because possible and impossible would be quite without meaning in such a setting. All the science fiction ever produced in the world would probably never equal the hidden reality of life and forms behind the incredible number of stars catalogued by our astronomers. If the reverse viewpoint is taken, one might suggest that it borders on disgraceful thinking to assume that our global village floats as a speck in a lifeless universe comprised of billions of dead galaxies.

Not only is our world physically part of the universe based on the marvellous equations of our astronomers, but our human adventure may be linked to other civilizations in the stars in the way this book attempts to show the historical relationship between the Earth and the Pleiades. This concept of the universe allows the traditional beliefs of mankind to be reinforced. Many of the myths and legends of the world, and the old themes of the apocryphal texts, the deluge and gods, probably contain a great deal of truth. The mating of the Taurus celestial, Poseidon, and the earth woman Cleito in the Atlantis account may be a common happening in the cosmos and part of fundamental laws of the universe for the survival of her species.

The Atlantis account could be veritable fact and the most valuable document we have of man and his universe. There are some strong points to substantiate this : to begin with the account was preserved in the oldest country in the world (Egypt) by sages of superior wisdom. It was then bequeathed to Greeks such as Solon and Plato, the greatest minds in antiquity, who would be the ultimate in relaying it to us in a coherent, historical manner.

This book makes four important discoveries that link the Atlantis story (the most fascinating tale ever told to mankind) to the Pleiades. The first is the word 'god' being applied to Poseidon which we associate in today's space age literature as 'extraterrestrial'. Second, the origins of this god are shown in the universe when his descendants on Earth worship him through a ceremony

10

involving a bull, the symbol of the Taurus constellation that contains the Pleiades. Third, that Poseidon as an extraterrestrial is a giant—"his own figure so tall as to touch the ridge of the roof". This fits perfectly with the Book of Enoch and the Bible that tells of giants being on earth in ancient times. These may be important keys to the mystery of Atlantis which could be the root of Western civilization. The fact that Atlantis has not been found should not detract from the story being worthy of consideration and this book brings forth evidence that Atlantis was in or near a city that rings with the interstellar sound of the Taurus constellation—Tarshish.

Most scholars of Atlantis throughout the centuries have completely ignored the ending. Most, I suspect, thought it was too incomprehensible and were embarrassed by it. Even if they took it seriously the best they could have done was to write it off as mythology since it is only recently that we have begun to understand the universe. "Wherefore he assembled together all the gods, into the abode which they honour most, standing as it does at the centre of the universe, and beholding all things that partake of generation; and when he assembled them he spake thus:" [Plato]

This description corresponds ideally to our theory of a universe that generates infinite forms of life. The pulsars are mystifying astronomers because of the synchronized signals they send from outer space suggesting superior intelligence behind them. Incredibly, the pulsars all seem to be the same age—2,000,000 years old. If they were in a cluster one could give credence to them being the same age, but since they are spread throughout our galaxy our imagination is given its severest shock. Another interesting concentration of pulsars is situated along the plane of the galactic equator.

One might be justified in asking which is more incredible: the long regarded mythical ending of 'Atlantis' or the stark reality of what our telescopes are actually seeing. Theories of the pulsars are in complete harmony with the Atlantis ending and superior beings in the universe. The pulsars may be navigation beacons

11

for space convoys, lighting pathways to galactic cities and the mysterious centre of the universe mentioned at the end of the Atlantis account. This reads like science fiction but it could be truth; truth is always beyond fiction. Science fiction is only the forerunner of truth. It was the science fiction writers and cartoonists who initiated our present space age, and now the reality of that age is beyond some of their wildest dreams.

Perhaps it will not be until the twenty-fifth century that the end of Atlantis is understood. The sources of the Atlantis account are Plato via Egypt. The origins of the Atlantis account are unknown. We should never lose sight of that fact. For all we know the original writers of the account may have been celestials from outer space, and the only ones capable of understanding the ending. We will elaborate further on the Atlantis ending in our chapter "Our Record of a Speech given in the Pleiades" and present a theory that Atlantis was initiated by the Pleiades through Poseidon and was ended by the Pleiades through Zeus. The few sentences at the end of Atlantis may be serving as a magic prism into the cosmos showing how some of its creatures are constructed and organized.

If our theories of the Atlantis account are correct it appears that the Earth and the Pleiades may be framed in a universe pulsating with life and communication. In following this line of reasoning I have found evidence of extraterrestrial visitations on Earth from the Pleiades. And this evidence is found in excellent sources—ancient scripture, the world's greatest literature, the discoveries of famous archaeologists, and above all, the megalithic structures still standing that the Taurus giants may have left when they were on Earth. They dramatically placed their mark on the Earth's civilization, and the bull, emblem of the Taurus constellation, suddenly appeared all over the world.

*ONE*

# The Pleiades (Taurus)

A GOOD PART of the secret of Man's evolution may lie in a beautiful cluster of stars called the Pleiades—400 light years from earth. They are in the constellation of Taurus and easy to find without the aid of a telescope.

The Pleiades and their constellation Taurus are deeply imbedded in the world's history and institutions to a degree that suggests this area of the sky may be linked to this planet in broader dimensions than the small rays of starlight it shines upon Earth. In studying ancient literature there seems to be evidence that beings came out of the Pleiades and landed on our planet. It seems incredible to us at first, but may be elementary to a universe whose fundamental laws are the communication and intergalactic mixing of her species.

In the framework of our large galaxy these stars are close and the equivalent of our next-door neighbours. Compounding this, the enormity of stars in this cluster may have produced a large number of planets capable of evolving intelligent beings that progressed to the stage of making a voyage to our nearby shores. We have emphasized too much the possibilities of celestial visitations from our solar system, which so far has proven quite lifeless. The Pleiades, only a little further away in the scale of an infinite universe, may well be the system that sent forth cosmic initiators to earth.

There are approximately 250 stars which are considered as belonging to the Pleiades, but it is seven bright stars and at times a few companions that figure prominently in our traditions. It is legitimate to theorize that all these stars may contain a solar system even though these stars are younger than our sun. In a small telescope the Pleiades is one of the loveliest sights to be seen. The whole field of the telescope is blazing with stars in glorious profusion, in streams and loops and in all possible combinations. The Pleiades seem to be the first stars mentioned in astronomical literature appearing in Chinese annals of 2537 B.C. In later years they probably have been studied more than any other group.

Euripides, Sappho and Homer made reference to them. Hesiod called them Atlas born. We will see later that this statement is distorted through time. The Pleiades are not the descendants of Atlas. Atlas was a descendant of these stars and lived on earth! And later, in the literature of *The Rubá'iyàt* of the poet-astronomer Omar Khayyám in 1123, the tent maker of Naishapur, "who stitched the tents of science", they were referred to as the Begetters, as beginning all things. This book will attempt to elaborate on this extremely powerful statement. Also they are intimately connected with traditions of the flood found among so many and widely separated nations, and especially in the Deluge Myth of Chaldea. We will attempt to show that the descendants of the Pleiades who came to Earth may have had a great deal to do with the causing of the flood.

Grecian temples were oriented to them, among which was the Great Parthenon. In the new world they were well-known objects in Mexico and South America. In ancient times they were a well-marked object of the Nile. Professor Charles Piazzi Smyth suggested that the seven chambers of the Great Pyramid commemorate these seven stars. If he was right, it seems reasonable to add that the presently unknown builders of the Great Pyramid may have been from the Pleiades.

Savage tribes knew the Pleiades familiarly. The natives of the Society and Tonga Islands called the stars the little eyes. The Abipones of the Paraguay River called them their 'grandfather', and hold festivals at the reappearance of the Pleiades in May. Perhaps the term 'grandfather' is used because the older and wiser civilizations of the Pleiades once came to Earth and influenced these tribes. South American legends state the Pleiades were inhabited and sent 'gods' to Earth. The Mayas are alleged to be 'children of the Pleiades'. The Arabs fixed here the seat of immortality; so did the Berbers of northern Africa and, widely separated from them, the Dyaks of Borneo—all thinking them the central point of the universe. Until Copernicus in the sixteenth century man had always believed that the Earth was the centre of the universe. What possessed these ancient people to point to a select area of the sky, far beyond the Earth and its solar system, and proclaim it as the centre of the universe? Australian tribes to this day dance in honour of the 'Seven Stars' because they were good to the black fellows. Elsewhere, the origin of fire and the knowledge of rice, culture are traced to them.

The Tuaregs of the Sahara Desert are a fascinating group who share a worldwide series of legends concerning the Pleiades. The letters of their tribe seem to have many of the same letters found in the word Taurus. One wonders if such deep knowledge of the stars handed down by generations of primitive peoples in different parts of the world for thousands of years can surely have been obtained only from celestials in some long-vanished civilization who had superior knowledge to earth people. For example, the only astronomical devices possessed by the ancient Maoris were sticks placed in the ground, whereby the movements of certain stars could be observed by lining them up with the sticks; yet they knew of an excess of seven stars in the Pleiades—a starry cluster greatly venerated by these antique people.

Individuals with average eyesight can see six stars in the Pleiades. Above-average eyesight may see a seventh, but the ancient Maoris knew of 'several' stars in excess of the seven in the Pleiades. Only binoculars or a telescope will show this many.

Two texts, The Book of Enoch and the Atlantis account long taken as myths, offer important clues to our linkage with the Pleiades and the giant beings that came from there. However, the most powerful evidence we have of space visitations from the Pleiades is the symbol of the ancient bull—the sign of the Taurus constellation that contains the celebrated cluster known as the seven stars. It permeates the entire Western world and countless statues and artifacts have been found glorifying it. It is symbolic of the 'Cosmic Bull' of heaven and represents the deification of the Taurus constellation, the bull of the zodiac. The Pleiades by themselves and the allegoric number seven pertaining to them are also deeply imbedded with profundity in our history and institutions. No doubt some of this interest was generated solely on the aesthetic appearance of the seven stars and their relationship to seasons, but further study of the subject seems to reveal a great deal more.

In 1940, Professor Marcel Homet, the great German archaeologist, made discoveries concerning the Pleiades in South America. Amongst his finds was the inscription of the bull-head on stones. He found the figure of bulls on a disc that seems to show the setting up of a theocratic government to natives. The bulls are probably symbolic of Pleiades celestials. Some of his other finds connected the Pleiades to Poseidon, the God of the Atlanteans. The ancient bull also has deep roots in the Atlantis story. The descendants of Poseidon worshipped him through the ceremony of the bull:

> In the sacred precincts of Poseidon there were bulls at large; and the ten princes being alone by themselves, after praying to the God that they might capture a victim well pleasing unto him, hunted after the bulls with staves and nooses but with no weapon of iron; and whatsoever bull they captured they led up to the pillar, and cut its throat over the top of the pillar, raining down blood on the inscription. And inscribed upon the pillar, besides the laws, was an oath which invoked mighty curses upon them that disobeyed. [Plato]

The god Poseidon was from the constellation of Taurus, the bull, and his descendants on Atlantis worshipped him through the bull animal symbolizing his origins in the universe. The blood from the sacrificial bull is symbolically running down sacred inscriptions handed down to us from the Taurus constellation. The ancient bull was not worshipped because prehistoric peoples glorified farm animals. The ancient bull was worshipped because it was symbolic of Taurus, the 'Bull of the Zodiac'.

The source of the Atlantis story is Plato via Egypt. The origin of the Atlantis story is unknown. Such is the context in which Atlantis exists. We should never lose sight of it. The account may have been bequeathed to us by celestials who meant it to be viewed in the perspective of the cosmos. Plato may have known this since he placed the account in *Timaeus* which is a work of the universe. Atlantis removed from the confines of Earth and placed in the universe flares from the smouldering ashes of Earth's mythology to brilliant flames of cosmic wisdom.

Seen in this new perspective the god Poseidon and the bull ceremony become more meaningful in outer-space connotations. And above all the ending of Atlantis becomes the most intellectually thrilling statement ever given in the field of literature.

From our new vantage point we see the importance of the opening of Atlantis:

> Like as we previously stated concerning the allotments of the Gods, that they portioned out the whole earth, here into larger allotments and there into smaller and provided for themselves shrines and sacrifices even so Poseidon took for his allotment the island of Atlantis. [Plato]

What else can this be but extraterrestrials landing on Earth and deciding to divide our planet amongst themselves? And when Plato mentions later the deification of Poseidon through the worship of the bull, where else could they have been from except the constellation of Taurus the Bull?

Our problem may no longer be the speculation of whether or not celestials were here. Further examination of the Atlantis account given to Plato, the overwhelming evidence of the ancient bull, and the electrifying discoveries of Professor Homet may reveal that they were here and where they were from. The distant future may develop a new theory of evolution that will link man historically, culturally and anthropologically to the Pleiades. A good part of the missing link so much sought after and never found by Darwin and others might lie in this select cluster of beautiful stars.

TWO

# The Pleiades—Seven Sisters in the Sky

THE CONSPICUOUS groups of stars in the sky such as the Great Bear, the Pleiades, and Orion's Belt consist for the most part of exceptionally massive stars which move in regular, orderly formation through a mixture of slighter stars. The stars of any one group such as the Pleiades not only show the same physical properties, but also have identical motions through space, thus coursing perpetually in the heavens in one another's society. Such a system is known by astronomers as a star cluster.

As stated in the last chapter there are 250 stars in the Pleiades but the most celebrated are the seven stars we immediately see representing the cluster. The names of these seven Pleiades stars are beautiful : Alcyone, Maia, Electra, Merope, Taygeta, Celaeno and Sterope. Hesiod called them the Seven Virgins and Virgin Stars; and Hesperides, the title of another set of Atlas's daughters from Hesperis, has been applied to them. Milton called them the Seven Atlantic Sisters. Some in ancient times knew them as the Sailor's Stars, but as the Seven Sisters they are familiar to most; and as the Seven Stars they appear in various Bible versions. We have noted the importance of this in Chapter 14 'The Pleiades and the Bible'.

In China they were worshipped by young girls and young women as the Seven Sisters of Industry, and in ancient times were known as Mol, the constellation or gang. Greek mythology mentions Pleione as mother of the seven sisters. Aeschylus assigned

18

the daughters' pious grief at their father's labour (Atlas) in bearing the world as the cause of their transformation and subsequent transfer to the heavens.

Their names have been recorded by Aratus :

> These are the seven names they bear :
> Alcyone, and Merope, Celaeno,,
> Taygeta, and Sterope, Electra,
> and queenly Maia, small alike and faint,
> But by the will of Jove illustrious all.

There is the well-known legend of the Lost Pleiade, according to which one of the seven sisters does not shine as brightly as the others. Greek myth accounts for this by saying that the faded star is Electra, who hid her face at the burning of Troy that was founded by her son Dardanos. She apparently has recovered from her sorrow and shines as bright as her sisters. Others say that Merope is the Lost Pleiade, who married a mortal while her sisters married gods. However, much of the mystery was solved when it was found that the seven stars were veiled in nebulous forms drifting around the stars and filling the spaces between with filmy star mist and sheets of stellar glaze. Thus we have Tennyson's descriptive passage :

> Many a night I saw the Pleiades rising through the mellow shade,
> Glitter like a swarm of fireflies tangled in a silver braid.

According to the German astronomer Bessel, the Pleiades are literally a cluster of suns drifting together in one direction. Some stars are floating slowly and others are advancing swiftly.

Alcyone is the brightest of the Pleiades and has generally been taken as the leading star. The early Arabs called it Al Jauzah or Al Wasat, the central one. Hiparchos alluded to it as the brightest one of the Pleiad. Alcyone shines to its sister stars with eighty-three times the brilliance of Sirius, and its brilliancy is one thousand times greater than that of our sun. A little triangle of stars near the bright Alcyone is especially attractive.

Alcyone was at one time thought to be the central star of the universe, around which all the galaxies revolved. However, this theory advanced by Dr Madler is no longer accepted due to the advance of modern-day astronomy.

Archibald Lampman paid the following tribute to Alcyone :

> ... the great and burning star,
> Immeasurably old, immeasurably far,
> Surging forth its silver flame
> through eternity ... Alcyone!

Maia has been known as personifying all the Pleiad stars, and ancient poets have cautioned the farmer against sowing his grain at the time of its setting. Legend says she was the first born and most beautiful of the sisters, and some have said that her star was the most luminous of the group. The nebula attached to this star, as part of the general nebulosity that envelops the group, was noticed in 1882 by Pickering and Henry.

Taygeta, a name famous in the Spartan story for the mother of Lacedaemon by Zeus, was mentioned by Ovid and Virgil as another representative of this stellar family, and was used to fix the two seasons of honey harvest. Celaeno or Celeno gives but one half the light of Taygeta but can be seen with the naked eye if a good one. Sterope I and Sterope II are a widely double star at the upper edge of the rising cluster, and faintly visible only by reason of the combined light. Merope is enveloped in a faintly extended, triangular, nebulous haze visually discovered by Tempel in October 1859; and there is a small distinct nebula, discovered by Barnard in November 1890, close by Merope almost hidden in its radiance, although intrinsically very bright. These nebulae are especially beautiful, resembling the fibrous cirrus clouds of fair weather.

The English astronomer Isaac Roberts (1829–1904) first discovered that the Pleiades cluster was enmeshed in a cloudy, filamentous cloud. It was taken as a cloud of dust that reflected the starlight it received. In his *Atlas of the Milky Way*, Barnard wrote: "One startling fact brought out by the study of these photographs is that the Pleiades, and their involved nebulosities, are but the central condensation of an enormous nebula, intricate in details and covering at least 100 square degrees of the sky."

The denser parts of the nebulosity are seen in the region of the brighter stars, and the long parallel filaments are particularly conspicuous over Merope. We might suppose that the Pleiades were born as a group from the same cloud. Their closeness to each other seems to indicate a common origin. It is still a mystery to astronomers why the majority of stars in the universe are not grouped in clusters but isolated in space.

The star Atlas was added to the group in ancient times and was known as Atlas, father of the seven daughters. Potter's translation of Euripides states: "Atlas, that on his brazen shoulders rolls yon heaven, the ancient mansion of the gods." This could be taken as recognition by the ancients that the celestials dwelt in the universe. With Pleione Atlas marks the handle of the Pleiad dipper, and is alleged to have a small close companion, said to have been discovered by Struve in 1827, and again revealed, at an occultation of the moon, on 6 January 1876.

The head of Taurus appears south-east of the Pleiades, and is below them in its rising. It is plainly marked by the fine V-shaped cluster Hyades. Worthy of note is the bright reddish star at the end of the southern arm of the V, which represents the bull's fiery eye. It is Aldebaran, 'the follower', so named because it rises soon after the Seven Sisters and pursues them across the heavens. Aldebaran is very nearly a standard first magnitude star.

Somewhere amongst the seven stars or the 250 others belonging to the cluster is probably a solar system containing a planet or planets that brought Poseidon and a contingent of giants to our planet. It may be worthy of consideration that Atlas and his daughters are not mythical characters who take the imaginary form of the Pleiades but real people who lived on Earth, and descendants of Poseidon. We are not told in the Atlantis account that Atlas had daughters but it is not unreasonable to assume that he could have. We speculate further that after their death the earth people enshrined Atlas and his offspring in the Pleiades, the place of their origins through Poseidon. Greek mythology connects Poseidon to the star Alcyone which may be a faint clue that he is connected to this star through its solar system. Unfortunately we are in the area of prehistory and will have to keep searching for more evidence.

Maia was said to be the first born and most beautiful of the sisters. In real life she could have been the first born of Atlas on Atlantis. And we recall that Ovid called her Atlantis making us believe she was connected to this region. In another chapter we will find that her name comes up a great deal in Africa, and Atlantis may have been in or near that area of the world. If Atlas and his descendants were the first royal blood line created on this planet from the Pleiades, then it could be for this reason that he and his immediate offspring are enshrined in this select cluster of stars and not for mythical reasons. This will be elaborated upon in future chapters.

We owe many of our clues concerning our historical linkage to the Pleiades from the Egyptians and their Atlantis story and the Greeks and their mythology probably based on real events in prehistory; much of our astronomical knowledge of the Pleiades is owed to the French :

Two French astronomers Paul and Prosper Henry ushered celestial photography into the nineteenth century. They were working at the Paris Observatory at the time astronomers were interested in discovering minor planets. To assist them the Henry brothers drafted detailed maps in zodiac areas. Their work was started in 1873 and was strictly visual. However, when they reached the area of the zodiac splitting the Milky Way the stars were so immense they had to resort to photography. In 1885 they obtained striking results on one of their first plates of the Pleiades. The beautiful stars revealed themselves in a vast nebula invisible to the naked eye. This was the first nebula discovered by photography.

Another feature was discovered. The Pleiades exploded into twice as many stars as shown on previous maps. The Paris Observatory became enthusiastic and planned an International Carte du Ciel. In 1887 a congress of international astronomers met in Paris to plan the execution of a photographic map of the sky. Twenty-one observatories around the world shared the work, and millions of new stars were discovered and catalogued. The project was immense and involved the work of generations of astronomers. This celestial photography has greatly aided the understanding of the motions of stars*

The organization of the Carte du Ciel established photography officially as a means of studying the sky. It marks the beginning of the contemporary period of astronomy and it was brought about through the inspiration of the Pleiades. We will try to convey through our theories that the Pleiades have influenced us to an even greater extent.

* See *The Discovery of the Universe* by Gerard de Vaucouleurs.

## THREE

# Crete: Earth's Generator of Taurus Culture

IN THE BLUE sparkling waters of the Mediterranean, south-east of the Greek mainland, lies an archaeologists' paradise — the ancient island of Crete. The island had hardly been touched by shovels until Arthur Evans began digging into its past. Whatever his intuition may have told him, it is doubtful if Evans knew that he may have been discovering symbols of the Taurus constellation and thereby unlocking Earth's door to the cosmos. However, it will be many years before Minoan civilization is fully understood, and placed in its true perspective in the universe.

Greek lore is full of wondrous tales of this cosmic island—most so fantastic they had long been considered myths. Homer's *Odyssey* is a saga of celestials taken as gods, goddesses, heroes and heroines. Rather than being an imaginative poet, Homer was probably in touch with great dimensions of the universe. Archaeologists have ignored Homer's geography, historians his historical truth, taking it as far-fetched; yet Homer more than once had been a reliable guide in the past. Near Crete at Delos is said to be where the new world started. However, little archaeological work had been done in these areas before Schliemann's and Evans' time.

Certain areas around the Mediterranean seem to ring with words that show an influence of the Taurus constellation—the Taurus Mountains, the legends of Tartarus, the ancient cities of Tarshish or Tartessos, the Tuareg tribe and the sacred scriptures

24

of the Torah, etc. The number seven constantly appears in this area's myths, literature, and religion, which possibly alludes many times in allegory to the seven Pleiades stars.

That the symbol of the Taurus or cosmic bull played a major role in the Mediterranean culture cannot be overemphasized. In this regard, one of the key finds that Evans found on Crete was its central palace of architectural brilliance. It was as big as Buckingham Palace in London, and had modern-day splendour —bathrooms with ingenious sanitary arrangements, drains and ventilators, conduits for water, and other noteworthy engineering accomplishments. The palace had not been in use since about 1400 B.C., even though vivid paintings showed life in a modern way depicting nobles of the court at the theatre, at feasts, at sports and at parties. The men were athletic in appearance and the women were in stylish looking gowns.

Clearing away the debris from the rooms, faint outlines of frescoes began to appear through the haze of dusty ruins. A fresco of people in solemn procession suddenly took form, then another of a boy, others showing strange griffin-like creatures— then suddenly a great painting of a bull.

More exploration revealed bulls on walls, on seal rings, carved into blocks of stone, until Evans exclaimed: "What a part these symbols play here." Meanwhile at Tiryns, Schliemann had found a painting of a huge bull with someone clinging to its horns.

If Homer held any truth, book nineteen of the *Odyssey* described a Crete which could have been great centuries before, perhaps even in the time period of Atlantis. If this theory holds any truth, then it can be conjectured that after prehistoric Crete's fall from power, a dark age descended upon the Mediterranean world, a dark age that may have descended after the biblical flood or the destruction of Atlantis. In these ruins Evans was bringing to life prehistory and its relationship to the universe. In the places of worship the horns of a bull were usually displayed on altars, indicating that they were part of profound ritualism. This cosmic symbol even forms the ornament of the great staircase of the palace, looming as a large section of the overall design.

The primitive wall paintings at Catal Huyuk in Anatolia, dating back to the sixth millennium B.C., already showed men touching the horns of a colossal bull as though to receive its zodiacal significance. In the contemporary Bronze Age world a supreme sky god was often identified with the bull, and the Egyptian sacred Apis Mnevis bulls were greatly venerated. Pharaoh was identified with the cosmic bull of heaven.

The most important discovery was when Evans found parts of the bull-leaping fresco. It was restored by M. Guilbsion. Here may have been shown the germ of another truth behind the constellation of Taurus. This point may have been missed by scholars feasting their eyes on what seemed to be slim boy and girl acrobats grappling with allegedly farm stock animals. They marvelled at the way a boy and girl supposedly working as a team ran or danced up to the bull, then seized its massive horns. One somersaulted over his back into the waiting arms of a partner standing behind the charging beast.

One could hardly believe that the fresco has anything to do with circus performances. Human beings are usually not capable of feats such as this, particularly children. The fresco is not depicting any physical events that took place on Crete but is probably a message symbolizing the children of Earth in their linkage to the Taurus constellation. The revolving children around the symbol of Taurus, which happens to be a bull, has created a surface impression.

This is why in spite of the number of times that it was represented by painters and sculptors, leaping as it was supposed to be practised in an arena was not altogether easy for scholars to understand. Another great difficulty has been the fact that bulls charging and tossing in anger always move the head sideways. In the so-called bull game scenes the animals are holding their heads perfectly straight. In conclusion, there may never have been any games, only symbols of the Taurus constellation.

Other symbols of the Taurus constellation are abundant on Crete—one of the most powerful being the large sacred horns that face Mount Juktas from the Palace of Knossos, and other symbols of importance are found on the island as well: the figure eight believed to be a symbol of the universe or our galaxy, double-headed axes which perhaps symbolized the pioneering of two planets, one being Earth and the other the native planet of the celestials of the Pleiades. And the snake which could represent coiled energy in the universe. In ancient times the seven-headed snake represented the supreme deity manifesting through his gods or seven spirits, by whose aid he established his universe. (This could mean God manifesting himself through the Pleiades that brought forth celestial beings to establish the universe.)

There is exciting evidence that leads us to believe that the Pleiades and Poseidon are connected to this region. It is the disc of Phaistos that was discovered in the Palace of Phaistos on the south of Crete. Commenting on the meaning of one of its inscribed symbols, Professor Marcel Homet the archaeologist states: "In any case, it should be noted that the Cabiri (Semitic for above), the circle with the seven dots, are associated both with the Pleiades and Poseidon, the god of the Atlanteans, whose capital city according to Plato bore his name."

Meanwhile the Palace of Minos stands stark today, once more looking over a landscape that may have been the dwelling place of cosmic initiators. The immense flight of stairs, decorated with huge Taurus bull's horns, once more sweeps up toward the heavens.

# FOUR

# Taurus, Atlantis, Crete—
# The Missing Links

THIS SCENE or a similar one could be the prologue to
Atlantis: A space ship leaves Taurus and passes through the
glowing swirls of nebulae that shroud the Pleiades and penetrates
the black tunnel leading to Earth. The ship continues its way
with the quiet hum of atomic engines. Now it presents a magnificent sight; contrasted in the darkness of space, sailing in a flood
of light like a queen who possessed the cosmos. On her decks are
celestials, amongst which is a giant by our standards. His name is
Poseidon, native of one of the many planets in the Pleiades. He is
of marvellous stature and beauty. His ship is travelling toward our
world and his final destiny will be the initiation of a new society
on the Earth island of Atlantis based on the precepts of cosmic
wisdom.

And so the stage is set for the most fascinating tale ever told to
mankind—the story of Atlantis. The story is preserved in Egypt
and works its way down through the ages, miraculously untouched
until it is presented to Plato in all the coherence of a historical
record. Examined in today's world it may very well be the most
reliable profile we have of an extraterrestrial living with us and
the most valuable document we have of man and the universe.

Poseidon's ship lands on Earth and after a meeting with the
celestials who accompanied him and in complete accordance with
*Timaeus*, the gods divide our world amongst themselves.
Poseidon's portion is the island of Atlantis. Poseidon settles in this

land and has contact with the natives. In the mountains near the plain lives Evenor, the earthman, his wife Leucippe and their only daughter Cleito. (In *Timaeus* Plato deems it necessary to separate his description of Poseidon by referring to Poseidon as a god and Evenor as "originally sprung from the earth".)

Poseidon would be in the realm of star masters with superior spirituality and knowledge of cosmic law; but he would not be immune from natural law. He must eat, drink, sleep, reproduce, and eventually complete the natural cycle on Earth as everyone else.

Through details that are missing, Poseidon as an extraterrestrial is capable of carrying out part of this cycle by successfully uniting with the earth woman Cleito. Poseidon falls in love with Cleito and marries her, thus creating the greatest romance story ever known to man on Earth. This is in keeping with the Book of Enoch that tells of giants having intercourse with earth women and siring giants. It also correlates with passages of the Bible— "and the sons of god found the daughters of men most fair"— "and there were giants in the earth in those days". It is also in keeping with Inca legends of giants descending from the clouds and having sexual intercourse with Inca women.

Ancient legends report that beings from the skies landed on Earth. These people were of excellent stature, marvellous beauty and gifted with transcendent wisdom. We are given a description of a family in Atlantis who had union with one of these celestials:

Thereon dwelt one of the natives originally sprung from the earth, Evenor by name, with his wife Leucippe; and they had for off-spring an only begotten daughter Cleito. And when this damsel was now come to marriageable age, her mother died and also her father; and Poseidon, being smitten with desire for her, wedded her. [Plato]

After his marriage he pioneers an island frontier on a planet that is new to him, carving out circular belts of sea and land for her protection. Poseidon is overly protective of Cleito and wants isolation apart from the others in order to carry out his plans with

29

her. This concept reminds us of the walled castles throughout the ages with royalty living inside. In fact, this may be the world's first record of royalty and how it came about.

The circular belts were to form the basis of a future city. It is natural that an extraterrestrial such as Poseidon would think of designing in terms of a circle. His circular designs could be representative of universal laws. The circle is represented in a great variety from the orbit of constellations to the structure of the atom. The square and triangle are seldom seen in a natural state and as far as we know the square is never found in nature except in the crystals of certain minerals. Circular movement is expressed in the grand cycle of the seasons, the laws of nature, the cycle of life, and the laws of the universe. These concentric island rings arranged by the Taurus god himself follow all the rules of a circular cosmogony :

. . . and to make the land whereon she dwelt impregnable he broke it off all round about; and he made circular belts of sea and land enclosing one another alternately, some greater, some smaller, two being of land and three of sea, which he carved as it were out of the midst of the island; and these belts were of even distances on all sides, so as to be impassable to man; for at that time neither ships nor sailing were as yet in existence. [Plato]

It is through this isolation of Cleito that we may have our first dramatic record of science on this planet. Poseidon might have used Cleito as part of a genetic programme in producing five pairs of twin sons, the first born being Atlas. This highly irregular and improbable birth code under normal conditions can be best explained in this way. Poseidon may have programmed these sons in this way in order to help him pioneer a new planet. This could explain why the first born, Atlas, was glorified throughout the ages more than his brothers because he signified the first born from the Pleiades who must shoulder the burden of the world. This may be why he is often depicted in the symbolism of our planet on his shoulders, and the word Atlas has so many global connotations. *Timaeus* states that the Atlantic ocean was named after him.

Poseidon's sons ruled Atlantis, and :

so all these, themselves and their descendants dwelt for many generations bearing rule over many other islands throughout the sea, and holding sway besides, over the Mediterranean peoples as far as Egypt and Tuscany. The wealth they possessed was so immense that the like had never been seen before in any royal house. [Plato]

During this age of splendour a magnificent temple was dedicated to Poseidon. And in its interior there was a golden statue that may have commemorated his voyage to earth from the Pleiades. This was depicted by the Taurus god standing on a chariot and driving six winged steeds—a fitting symbol for any astronaut or celestial who came to earth. "And they placed therein golden statues, one being that of the god standing on a chariot and driving six winged steeds." [Plato]

This passage also gives us a physical description of Poseidon, this mysterious personage whose origins are 400 light years from Earth : "his own figure so tall as to touch the ridge of the roof." [Plato]

If the sculptors were keeping their sense of proportion, and we might assume they were since nothing unusual is mentioned concerning the nereids and dolphins, then the central figure of the statue is modelled after a giant.

If Poseidon is a giant it might be what we would expect, a being like ourselves but proportionate to a different sized planet than our own in the Pleiades. Ancient scripture makes great reference to giants on Earth in prehistoric days. If the Pleiades are connected to our Earth through Poseidon and Atlantis, then the exciting thing for us to do is try to find Atlantis. Scholars have paid particular attention to Crete because of its ancient bull culture.

Artifacts have revealed religious practices in the Aegean—the worship of a mother goddess, a boy god and the bull sacrifice—a similar theme to the Atlantis account. The mother goddess could be Cleito, the boy god Atlas and the bull ceremony of which we are now familiar. Evans thought the goddess was connected to King Minos, long associated with the area. One wonders if

31

the original Minos and Poseidon's son Mneseus were one and the same since the Atlantis account mentions he was one of the sons who had sway over the Mediterranean. The connection Evans was looking for may have been between Cleito and Mneseus as mother and son.

Professor Frost had in 1909 noticed similarities between Minoans and Atlanteans. Minoan culture does correlate in some ways with the Atlantean description. The harbours, for example, with their shipping and merchants coming from all ports, the elaborate palace found by Evans, and the deification of the bull, are all typically, but not exclusively, Minoan.

Plato's account of Atlantis, from Egyptian priests and brought to Greece by Solon, includes a geographical description of an antediluvian world. It tells of a conflict between the Atlanteans and the prehistoric Greeks. After the Atlanteans are defeated in battle, their island sinks beneath the sea and the army of the Greeks is swallowed by the land. The magnitude of these catastrophes leads us to believe that larger dimensions such as celestial intervention could have been worked in with the battles.

The Mediterranean references throughout the Atlantis story should strongly suggest that Atlantis was in or near to that area. However, many world scholars have placed Atlantis far from the Mediterranean in other recondite areas of the world. The Atlantic ocean has been a favourite location because the transmission says it was beyond the Pillars of Heracles.

Discouraging to those who would have Atlantis in the mid-Atlantic are the remarks of Dr. Galanopoulos, one of the world's experts on Atlantis. He states that amongst oceanographic data that are constantly being augmented as research ships of many nations sample the ocean bottom nothing has been found. The mid-Atlantic ridge, on which lie the Azores, often associated with Atlantis, has been dated radiologically and no evidence was found for sunken islands in the last 72,000 years. The thickness of the earth's rocky crust is greater under the continents than under the oceans. At a location beneath the mid-Atlantic ridge near the Azores, the earth's crust has been found to be much thinner than that under the continents. This indicates that an Atlantean continent in this area is all but impossible.

Dr. Galanopoulos believes that Atlantis was in Crete. He has a theory for Atlantis not fitting in Crete because there was a ten fold discrepancy in the translation. In the translation of the Egyptian scripts by Solon, the symbol representing 100 was unquestionably rendered as 1,000. An example of this same sort of confusion in modern times is the contrast between the American billion, which is a thousand million, and the English billion, which is a million million. This theory cuts all the figures used in Atlantis to 1/10 of their value, and subsequently Atlantis would fit in Crete.*

Dr Galanopoulos believes that Plato was confused by the enormous figures of Atlantis and was forced to put Atlantis outside the Pillars of Heracles because it would not fit in the Mediterranean, and had he known of such things as the Thera eruption he would have favoured Crete. It is my view that Plato had nothing to do with the contrivance of the Atlantis story in any way and only gave us a pure recital from Egyptian sources and unknown origins. His only action was inserting the work as it stood into *Timaeus*. However, I am the first to admit that at times some of the figures pertaining to Atlantis can be somewhat disturbing.

In leading expeditions to these regions Dr Galanopoulos found similarities to the Atlantis story. Among discoveries was red and black lava rock found on the island of Thera which coincides with Plato's description of red and black stones on Atlantis; and murex shells that excrete purple dye, believed to be the colour of the robes used by the Atlantean princes.

My own view is that Dr Galanopoulos is close to the Atlantis influence with his interest in the 'cosmic' island of Crete. Ancient Crete was part of the Atlantean empire in prehistoric times; but I believe if you are looking for the source of Atlantis you have to explore the north-west African regions and the regions of Spain close to the Pillars—the area said to be ruled by Poseidon's son Gadeirus. The nearby mountains in Morocco were believed by the ancients to be named after Atlas. An electrifying find was made in Agadir in Morocco where the French captain La Fanechere discovered a complete arsenal of hunting weapons

---

* *Voyage to Atlantis* by James W. Mavor.

including 500 double-edged axes weighing 17½ pounds, or twenty times as heavy for you and I. It has been estimated that to handle the axe one would have to have hands of a size equal to a giant with a height of at least 13 feet. La Fanechere may have discovered the implements of the Taurus giants in or near Atlantis regions. And further up the coast is an ancient city that may be the source of Atlantis itself. A city that rings with the interstellar sound of the Taurus constellation—Tarshish!

# FIVE

# *Taurus Tartessos Atlantis*

"WHILE the sea-way and largest harbour were filled with ships and merchants coming from all quarters, which by reason of their multitude caused clamour and tumult of every description and an unceasing din night and day."

The ear splitting clangour of the Atlantean harbour reverberates through this passage from Plato. The account states that before the arrival of Poseidon ships and sailing were not in existence. In the dawn of prehistory sleeping villages of primitive men were scattered throughout the stillness of our world; in isolation waiting for the reverie of Poseidon and other celestials to wake them in the dawn of a new civilization. The above passage shows the climax of that cosmic initiation. Merchant ships are generating trade and commerce from Atlantis.

Where was this harbour that seems to be generating so much influence? The prehistoric regions of Tarshish or Tartessos in south-western Spain, near Cadiz may be close to the Atlantis source. Like Atlantis it greatly influenced large regions of the Mediterranean through its wealth and power. The passage in Isaiah 23 : 10 describing Tyre as one of its offspring suggests it might have been the original initiator of Mediterranean civilizations. "Pass through thy land as a river, O *daughter* of Tarshish : there is no more strength."

We learn in Ezekiel 27 : 12 that Tarshish supplied wealth to the Mediterranean : "Tarshish was thy merchant by reason of the multitude of all kinds of riches; with silver, iron, tin and lead they traded in thy fairs". Isaiah 23 : 10 1. suggests its traffic on the broad expanse of the Mediterranean : "Howl ye ships of Tarshish".

35

We learn in Kings 10:22 that King Solomon traded with Tarshish: "For the King at sea had a navy at Tarshish, bringing gold and silver, ivory and apes and peacocks." And 10:23: "So king Solomon exceeded all the kings of the earth for riches and for wisdom." The interior roof of the temple of Poseidon in Atlantis was ivory, varigated with gold and silver. Solomon may have been trading with the Atlantean regions. In the Tarshish area there is still a mining town with the name Tharsis and the Rio Tinto copper mines of which they are a part are estimated at 8,000 to 10,000 years old.

L. Sprague de Camp points out in *Lost Continents, the Atlantis Theme*, that the origins of the word Tartessos are uncertain: "The name of the place sounds like some of those applied to the Etruscans, whom the Greeks called Tyrrenhoi and the Egyptians called Tursha, and who were said in classical times to be from Lydia. The Etruscans, though called themselves Rasena, which sounds nothing like Tartessos."

Perhaps the words Tarshish and Tartessos are connected to Taurus—the origins of the words being in the constellation itself. This may not be so extreme as it first sounds. Words in our vocabulary may have their origins in space. The Atlantis account suggests that Poseidon named his second eldest son in the native Atlantean language. If Poseidon issued the word "Gaderius" from his own tongue as the account suggests and our Poseidon – Pleiades theories are correct we have in our possession a word originating 400 light years from earth.

Leaving our theories in the realm of the cosmos we return to Europe and wonder if Tarshish is the source of Atlantean culture. Strabo tells us the Carthaginians found the natives of Tarshish using silver for feeding troughs and wine jars (see end of chapter). We wonder further if this was the region that spawned the glittering silver palaces of Atlantis and Homer's Phaecia. Was it here that Odysseus walked with Pallas Athene in Book 7 of the *Odyssey*? It is on these pages that we are given a vivid description of Odysseus walking amidst Phaecian sailors. He marvels at their harbours, pallisades and meeting places for sea lords—all of which may be a further amplification of Plato's quote opening this chapter.

After walking through the Phaecian water front Odysseus approaches the palace of Alcinous. He sets foot on a bronze threshold and sees a great radiance lighting up the high roofed halls. The interior has walls of bronze adorned with golden doors hung on posts of silver. The lintels of the doors are also silver. There were statues of gold and silver dogs amidst silver thrones. A maid gave Odysseus a silver basin to wash his hands. Ivory, gold and silver were the themes of the temples of Atlantis.

Book 7 mentions winter and summer, orchards and gardens exactly as described in Atlantis. Similar to Atlantis there are two springs, one supplying the palace and the other the townfolk. Poseidon's descendants surround his two springs with edifices similar to the palace of Alcinous.

One wonders if it was in Tarshish that Odysseus had his audience with the sea captains of the Phaecians (Atlanteans?) begging for his passage home as stated by Homer. And if this meeting took place in Plato's prehistoric harbour. Did immortals such as Poseidon descend here from heaven as suggested in the same chapter and initiate the silvery kingdom that was Atlantis? Book 7 is one of the most fascinating sections of the Odyssey. It may be giving us a photographic description of Tarshish or Atlantis under the guise of Phaecia.

Mrs Wishaw, a past director of the Ango-American Spanish School of Archaeology, held the theory that the Tarshish regions near modern day Cadiz was a colony of Atlantis and not Atlantis itself. Adhering to the exact words of the account, she sites Poseidon's son Gadeirus who inherited that part of the kingdom beyond the Pillars of Heracles and ruled at Gadeira.

The word Cadiz may have its origins with "Gadeirus". It can be traced to Gades (Cadiz), the same root word Agadir in Morocco and Gadeirus. She believed that Atlantis sent forth the Tarshish–Tartessos colony. If she is right it is in keeping with the Atlantis account which states that Poseidon designated a ruling area to his second eldest son, Gadeirus. Her conclusions were further substantiated by the evidence of neolithic workings of the Rio Tinto mines and of skilled hydraulic engineering at Niebla and Rhonda in the early copper age.

Mrs Wishaw found evidence in the Tartessos region of a Libyan–Tartessian culture. She compared the manners, culture and religions of Tartessians and Libyans and believed they had a common origin in the west. She discovered a sun temple lying $60\frac{1}{4}$ metres below the Calle Abades in Seville. The sun symbol is often associated with Atlantis, and this labyrinth structure has a circular tomb sealed by a great monolith, and a roof delicately constructed to allow the sun's rays to penetrate. One wonders if this edifice is not a reflection of the celestial kingdoms of Poseidon. A corresponding chapel vault on the other side of the temple constructed with material similar to the Queen's Tower at Niebla, dates the sun structure as neolithic, if not earlier, possibly capturing the Atlantean age. Mrs Wishaw believed that the remnants of Tarshish–Tartessos were hidden under the streets of Seville.

Mrs Wishaw believed that the Atlantis account was worthy of corroboration and the strong association of Poseidon's son Gadeirus with her regions of exploration added to her convictions. She also found a neolithic cup near Seville, engraved with the picture of a woman fighting two Libyan warriors; prehistoric Iberian graves; and modern customs alluding to an ancient matriarchal society like that of the Berbers. Evidence of matriarchal societies has been found throughout the Mediterranean that could have originated from the deification of Cleito, the great earth mother who mated with the Taurus celestial, Poseidon and brought forth the ten royal lines, and a new variation of human life on our planet.

Unfortunately the origins of these great mysteries have not been found and Tarshish–Tartessos itself evades discovery. Even so, it should be pointed out that large building blocks have been discovered underground in silted soil, too near the water level for practical excavation. The closest approach to the site of Tarshish may have been by Schulten, Bonsor and Jesssen. They excavated a block of masonry that seemed to depict two ancient cities, but high water levels allowed only surface digging. These imaginative explorers were forced to admit that the Atlantean remains of Tarshish could have sunk in the depths of some unknown geological past. The truth of the Homeric legends and the cosmic secrets of the Atlantis mystery may lie in the mud of the Guadalquiver estuary surrounding the regions.

Nearby the Temple of Melkarth of Gades was discovered by Schulten. In its ruins were two wells reminding us of the two springs that course around Poseidon's Atlantean temple and the Phaecian palace of Alcinous in the *Odyssey*. Schulten's theory substantiated by Richard Hennig was that all the necessary essentials for the Atlantis account were echoed in these regions.

Our ancient literature may be holding important clues of this paradisaic Eden of the west but our archaeological evidence is sparse. One of the few things found was a ring discovered by Schulten in 1923. It has an inscription that has not yet been deciphered. The unknown letters may contain important clues to the mysteries of Tarshish–Tartessos.

With its unknown origins Tarshish surfaced and flourished into the period of our recorded history as a wealthy trading and mining area. When the Phoenicians arrived in 1000 B.C. they found silver so abundant they had trouble carrying it away. This correlates with Book 7 of the *Odyssey* when Odysseus encounters so many silver objects and the silvery temples of Atlantis. It is even alleged that the Phoenician sailors used heavy Tarshish silver as anchors for their cargo galleys. The Carthaginians even found the natives using silver for feeding troughs and wine jars.

Out of all the global locations for Atlantis Tarshish seems the most promising and closest to the Atlantis source. Areas like ancient Crete were probably only reflections of the Atlantis empire. Actually, a marvellous piece of writing and masterpiece like the Atlantis account would not leave out the Atlantis location. The location of Atlantis is found in the description of the area ruled by the royal celestial sage, Gadeirus: "who had for his portion the extremity of the island near the Pillars of Heracles up to the part of the country now called Gadeira. . . ." This would explain why Atlantis was such a strong influence in the Mediterranean as the account states. Those who have sailed thousands of miles away from the pillars looking for Atlantis may have overlooked the extreme importance of these few words. Whether or not Tarshish was Atlantis or a portion ruled by Gadeirus may be irrelevant since it could be close enough to the Atlantean source to warrant consideration.

Tarshish according to Schulten and Mrs Wishaw went back to the neolithic age, and if this is so its history could capture the time period of Poseidon and his arrival from space and the Atlantis story that followed.

We learn from Polybius that the original Tarshish was on a large island near another island called Gades. The island description correlates with Atlantis. It is believed that ancient Tarshish was near the Baetis river, now the Guadalquiver. The river cut its way into ancient Hispalis now Seville. The region is now desolate and any trace of glorious empires has vanished.

If Atlantis was at or near Tarshish it is doubtful whether Plato could either compose this story from his imagination or the available knowledge of his day. The work is an exercise in memory as clearly stated by Critias who claimed he memorized the account from Solon. Even the contemporary Egyptian priests who gave the ancient story to Solon probably had little knowledge of the Tarshish regions.

There were only a few explorers in Plato's time that had ventured beyond the pillars. Skylax Karyanda, the Columbus of Plato's day wrote a navigational account of Gadeira, Tarshish and Kerne. However, the report was vague and far from lending itself as a foundation for which Plato could build an enormous Atlantean civilization comprised of many generations. The geographical knowledge of Plato, Critias and Solon were probably limited. From ancient Athens their vision of the area beyond the pillars would be misty. They were only Grecian marathon runners relaying one to the other the Egyptian torch spewing Atlantean flames. This will be elaborated upon in the next chapter.

As well as these suggestive undercurrents of prehistory we have

40

scatterings of the Tarshish regions in our recorded history. One of the first inhabitants in our records in the Turdetani or Turduli who had a high degree of civilization including an alphabet and ancient laws. Their history mentions Ethiopians in North Africa and the Atlas mountains. Homer talks of Ethiopians as "Athiopes" and suggests their location is in western regions. "Athiopes" may be a combination of Atlas–Merope. There was also a tribe in ancient times known as Meropids. More evidence perhaps of the Pleiades influence being in North Africa through Poseidon and his son Atlas. Merope is one of the Pleiades stars. Ethiopia, Scheria, Tarshish and Phaecia may have all been close to the Atlantis source. The theory has already been made by others that Atlantis and Scheria are memories of Tartessos-Tarshish. Homer describes Phaecia in the *Odyssey* as the land at the end of the world. The *Odyssey* says that Phaecians had great sea power. Harbours and the splendour of their city seems to equal Atlantis.

Mysteriously, our literature contains nothing of Tartessos after the Carthaginian era. What happened to this city that may contain so many important keys to the cosmic ignition of Western civilization? There are strong suspicions that the Carthaginian admiral Himilco obliterated its golden past but it is not entirely certain. Meanwhile we have the following valuable quotes from well-known historians :

I, 163 : now the Phokaians were the first of the Greeks to perform long voyages, and it was they who made the Greeks acquainted with the Adriatic and Trrhenia, with Iberia, and the city of Tartessos. The vessel they used in their voyages was not the round built merchant ship, but the long fifty-oared galley. On their arrival at Tartessos, the king of the country named Arganthonios, took a liking to them. This monarch reigned over Tartessians for eighty years, and lived to be 120 years old. He regarded the Phokaians with so much favour as, at first, to beg them to quit Ionia and settle in whatever part of his country they liked. . . .
IV, 152 : a Samian vessel under the command of a man named Kilaios . . . quitted the island; and, anxious to reach Egypt, made sail in that direction, but were carried out of their course by a gale from the east. The storm not abating, they were driven past the Pillars of Heracles, and at last by some special guiding

providences reached Tartessos. This trading town was in those days a virgin port, unfrequented by merchants. Hence the Samians made by the return voyage a profit greater than the Greeks before their day, excepting Sostratos, son of Laodamus.*

III, i, 6 : They call the country (of south-western Spain) Baetica after the river, and also Turdetania after the inhabitants; they call the inhabitants both Turdetanians and Turdulians . . . The Turdetanians are ranked as the wisest of the Iberians; and they make use of an alphabet and possess records of their ancient history, poems, and laws written in verse that are 6,000 years old, as they assert. And also the other Iberians use an alphabet though not letters of one and the same character, for their speech is not one and the same . . .

III, ii, 11 : Not very far from Castalo is also the mountain in which the Baetis is said to rise; it is called 'Silver Mountain' on account of the silver mines that are in it. . . . The ancients seem to have called the Baetis River 'Tartessos'; and to have called Gades and the adjoining islands 'Erytheia', and this is supposed to be the reason why Stesichoros spoke as he did about the neat herd of Geryon, namely that he was born "about opposite famous Erytheia, beside the unlimited silver-rooted springs of the river Tartessos, in a cavern of a cliff". Since the river had two mouths, a city was planted on the intervening territory in former times, it is said—a city which was called Tartessos, after the name of the river; and the country, which is now occupied by the Turdulians was called 'Tartessis'. Further, Eratosthenes says that the country adjoining Calpe is called 'Tartessis', and the Erytheia is called 'Blest Isle'. . . .

III, ii, 14 : The wealth of Iberia is further evidenced by the following facts : the Carthaginians who, along with Barcas, made a campaign against Iberia found the people in Turdentania, as the historians tell us, using silver feeding-troughs and wine-jars. And one might assume that it was either from their great prosperity that the people there got the additional name of 'Makraiones' ('Long-livers') and particularly the chieftains; and that this is why Anakreon said as follows : "I, for my part, should neither wish the horn of Amaltheia, nor yet to be king of Tartessos for one hundred and fifty years"; and why Herodotos recorded even the name of the king, whom he called Arganthonios. . . . Some, however, call Tartessos the Carteia of today.†

* Herodotus, *The Histories* (Rawlinson translation).
† Strabo, *Geography* (Jones-Sterret translation).

# SIX

# Atlantis—The Supreme Monument of the Mediterranean

THREE DIFFERENT narratives amongst others concerning the existence of the first humanity have reached the second: the Babylonian, repeated in the Book of Genesis, about the flood, the Book of Enoch telling of giants, and the Egyptian transmission relayed through Plato about Atlantis.

For twenty-five centuries scholars have been trying to solve the Atlantis account of the Egyptian priests about the origins of Western civilization and it is likely they will go on struggling with it for some time to come. Although keenly interested, most scholars throughout the ages have said it was myth. But what if they are wrong and Atlantis is history? What if Atlantis is the true account of how our Western civilization began, and this has been largely misunderstood because of semantics? It is only as we progress ourselves that the words in the Atlantis account take on new meaning. To a nineteenth-century man the word 'god' applied to Poseidon would mean a mythical character. To a twentieth-century man it could mean an extraterrestrial. Poseidon's five sets of twin sons would seem unnatural and unbelievable in a world living for centuries in a natural pastoral age. In a scientific age beginning to understand genetic engineering such a concept may not be so unnatural or unbelievable. The ending would be taken as pure fantasy throughout the ages and only slightly reveal itself factually as our twentieth-century telescopes begin to study pulsars. To twenty-fifth-century man exploring vast regions of space, the ending may seem basic as contact

43

is made with superior intelligences in the universe. Plato has been accused so often of being a myth-maker because of his Atlantis account that perhaps someone should rescue him.

The philosopher Aristokles the son of Ariston, better known by his nickname Plato, was the receiver of the Atlantis story— not its creator as scholars keep saying, nor even its historian in the strictest sense of the word, but its receiver from its ancient transmission in Egypt. Since Plato's reception nearly two thousand books and articles have been written about Atlantis. Some of these are flights of imagination; others are scientifically disciplined.

Explorers have travelled across vast regions looking for traces of Atlantean culture described by Egyptian priests, geologists have devoted years to finding out if continents and islands do rise and sink, and oceanographers have plunged into the murky depths of the seas for any visible remains. Clearly, along with the sceptics, many intelligent people in the world must believe that Atlantis existed even though the story has been largely taken as myth. There is no doubt that Atlantis enters the general problem of man and Western civilization, and in my view whether or not we are linked in our evolution to our galaxy, rather than just our planet —or perhaps even to our universe and beyond.

It may be that those answers can only be found by focusing on Plato's work as it stands, and gently putting aside many of the mythical works on Atlantis that are cluttering Plato's message from Egypt. We should keep studying the exact words in his report, and while we are in this new line of activity we should keep in mind the line in Desiderata: "and the universe shall unfold as it should".

And as it does Plato's message will take on new meaning.

Donnelly, for example, could not write a book such as this one because we are a product of the space age and he was not. And future generations will be able to understand Atlantis better than we. However, it wouldn't hurt to have a little background on Plato's report and discuss its validity.

Plato wrote *Timaeus* as a sequel to *The Republic*. Both in my view have undercurrents of cosmic influence. *Timaeus* is an exposition of the universe comprised of cosmology, physics and biology put into the mouth of the astronomer Timaeus of Locri. The discussion is introduced by the famous narrative of the gallantry of the prehistoric Athenians who defeated the kings of Atlantis in their ambitious attempt to conquer the Mediterranean. The story is elaborated in more detail in the *Critias* which is a sequel to *Timaeus*.

Critias is also the name of a character in *Timaeus*. In this work Critias tells how a century and a half before, the renowned Athenian statesman Solon heard the Atlantis story in Egypt, at Sais, the capital of King Ahmes. On his return to Athens he repeated it to his brother Dropides, Critias's great-grandfather, who in turn passed it on to his descendants, by which means Plato acquired it. It is here that sceptics of Atlantis make their strongest case—simply, that oral tradition is not the best form of authenticity. Admittedly, distortion does occur through such a process but we must remember that the story is not circulating to us through ale-house conversation but carefully handed on by the greatest minds in antiquity and on these grounds there may be a good chance that it is true. If it is true we will be fortunate, being able to use it as a key to understanding mythology, religion, anthropology, civilization, sociology, science and the universe. The ancients must have seen some truth in it as shown by their enthusiasm. Critias mentions that the story so interested him that he vividly memorized every word. Socrates believed him and was enthusiastic, believing the story was no prefabricated myth but genuine history.

In Egypt Solon got into an historical discussion with a group of priests of the goddess Neith or Isis whom the Greeks identified with their own Athena (possibly a celestial who accompanied Poseidon from Taurus). When Solon tried to impress them by telling them some of the Greek traditions, the oldest priest, named Sonchis according to Plutarch, admonished him. The Greeks were children he said because they remembered only one flood whereas there were many. He mentioned that mankind reaches a certain level of civilization and then is destroyed by a certain pestilence in heaven and only those destitute of letters are left to start a new wave of humanity. This could be one of the most thought-provoking statements ever given to man about his universe and is in harmony with the ending of Atlantis.

In one of the dialogues in *Timaeus*, Critias states that when the gods divided up the world, Athena and Hephaistos received Athens and set up the Athenian state similar to the ideal state of Plato's *Republic*. Here we see by our theories the celestials landing from the Pleiades, a meeting takes place and Athena is given the territory of Greece and Poseidon the administration of Atlantis. Scholars have largely taken the remarks in *Timaeus* as myth because there are no remains of a superior Greek culture in approximately 9560 B.C. However, the case is not closed and *Timaeus* may be giving us an exciting account of how Greece began. A vital fact also worth mentioning is that Plato received Atlantis and inserted it in *Timaeus* which is a work of the universe. By that course of action Plato might have realized that Atlantis and Greece had a much greater universal theme than we presently realize. Atlantis and the facts pertaining to it were probably intended by Plato to be viewed in the perspective of the universe.

*Timaeus* states there was a mighty empire of Atlantis, centring on an island west of the Pillars of Heracles (the Strait of Gibraltar), larger than Africa and Asia Minor combined and surrounded by smaller islands. However this still keeps Tarshish and its environs open for consideration because the word 'larger' comes from the Greek word 'meison' which can mean larger but also more powerful than.

In these ancient times you could traverse this great archipelago island by island and reach the super continent beyond Atlantis. This could apply to Tarshish and the surrounding continent could be the Americas. The Atlanteans, not satisfied with ruling their own islands, had tried to conquer the entire Mediterranean region. They had extended their rule as far as Egypt and Tuscany when they were defeated by the courageous Athenians. Then a great earthquake and flood devastated Athens, swallowed the Athenian army and caused Atlantis to sink in the turbulent waters of the Atlantic Ocean. For a great period of time afterwards the waters west of Gibraltar were unnavigable because of the shoals left by the sinking Atlantis.

Certain elements of Plato's report, even if not the story itself, do appear before Plato's time, such as the example we used in another chapter of Poseidon being worshipped in the Mediterranean long before Plato. Atlas was also an ancient figure of Greek myth and enshrined in the Pleiades with a star now bearing his name. Homer talks of him as "crafty Atlas who knows the depths of the whole sea, and keeps the tall pillars that keep heaven and earth asunder". This passage could mean that the Pillars of Heracles (Gibraltar) divide earth people and celestials from heaven such as Poseidon on Atlantis.

The poet Hesiod had Atlas supporting the heavens with his head and arms, and the Greek playwrights added the remark that Atlas was condemned by Zeus for his part in the Titan's rebellion to perform the exhausting work of the west :

> Where the Hesperides their song
> Attune : no mariner can thence prolong
> The voyage, for, his daring bark t'impede
>  Neptune those hallowed bounds mountains
> Where Atlas with unwearied toil sustains
>  The heavens' incumbent load.

The allusion here to the Hesperides may be a clue that Atlas is in the west. Later classical writers deciphered this myth by making Atlas a scholar king who founded the science of astronomy, and some theologians identified him with the biblical Enoch. If Atlas did found the science of astronomy he would be the ideal person to do it if he were the son of Poseidon, an extraterrestrial who had seen large areas of the universe first-hand. Atlas as half celestial would have superior intelligence in order to initiate such concepts to an earth society still destitute of letters. His genetic superiority may be also why we have records of him through legend establishing empires on Earth. The last line of the above poem could mean that the heavens (universe) have put pressure on Atlas being the first born of Pleiades stock on a new planet.

The Atlas myth seems to transcend far back in prehistory suggesting that Atlas could have been a real character in Atlantis as the prehistoric Egyptian account states. In fact, there is reason to believe that Atlas, having charge of the heaven-supporting pillars, existed in Greece centuries before the Greeks had any clear notion of the geography of the western Mediterranean. Ancient stories identifying him with a real mountain and placing him in the west could be based on fact.

The rivalry of Poseidon and Athena, which in the Atlantis account may take the form of the Atlanto–Athenian war, also goes back a long way. In the context of Greek myth, both Athena and Poseidon claimed Athens. Everything adjacent to the Atlantis transmission may not be totally or partly myth. In addition to Plato's relay, ancient scholars from Herodotus on down describe primitive tribes in north-west Africa, which they call Atlantes, Atarantes, or Atlantio, all names similar to Atlas. These may be clear facts that are important. According to this pioneering first-century historian, the Atlantio claimed that Atlas named both Mount Atlas and themselves after his own name.

Even though strong historical facts such as this exist, sceptics believe that Plato compounded ingredients from geographical, historical and mythical sources and formulated them to produce a fictional masterpiece—an approach, as every artist knows, the ultimate in the creative process. If their views are correct, then Plato is the greatest science-fiction writer of all time capable of producing a phantasmagoria that led many of the world's scholars to believe it was the root of Western civilization. Creativity of such magnitude has seldom been known. It is strange, then, that Plato was not known primarily as a creative person like Leonardo da Vinci but as one whose earliest ambitions were political followed by philosophical and scientific endeavours based on a strong emphasis of mathematics.

Clearly, Plato did not create Atlantis but repeated something far beyond himself, that we are just beginning to understand. It may be for this reason that it was not until three centuries after Plato's time that we get a recorded utterance from spellbound writers. Most were cautiously noncommittal and as would be expected the reaction was disbelief and confusion. Strabo was sceptical, thinking the ageing Plato must have been suffering from delusions. Without question scholars took it as a fiction and at best an allegory by which Plato meant to expound his social ideals.

The latter approach is quite in keeping with what we know of Plato's approach to such works as *The Republic* and his dialectics but it is out of context in the clear-cut historical style used in Atlantis. The fact that he is out of style in his Atlantis presentation suggests that he got it from someone else, and is only coherently relating it to us. This shows up when he doesn't understand the size of the megalithic trenches (probably built by giants) but is duty bound to tell us anyway :

> Now, as regards the depth of this trench and its breadth and length, it seems incredible that it be so large as the account states, considering that it was made by hand, and in addition to all the other operations, but, nonetheless we must report what we heard.

He also uses phrases such as : "We must endeavour next to repeat the account of the rest of the country."

Another point worth making is that Atlantis reads more like a photographic description from Plato's memory tract rather than a deep philosophical work. Morals, for example, are only briefly mentioned near the end of the recital when Atlantis is about to be destroyed.

There was a glimmer of credence when the church fathers along with the neoplatonists took the Atlantis transmission as authentic. Unfortunately, the rise of Christianity and the decline of the Roman Empire shifted intellectual interest from practical history to religious rituals. Even though *Timaeus* had been translated into Latin by Chalcidius, interest in Atlantis and other important events of the past declined.

Interest in Atlantis flared from smouldering embers with the discovery of the new world by Columbus, and since then has grown to a considerable extent. In 1553, the Spanish historian Francesco Lopez de Gomara in his general history of the Indes suggested that the Atlantis regions were in the newly discovered Americas. In 1580 the Englishman John Dee gave further strength to this theory by labelling America Atlantis on one of his maps. Later, in 1689 the French cartographer Sanson, and in 1769 Robert de Vangoudy, published maps of America showing how Poseidon divided the land amongst his ten sons. The America Atlantis theory drew considerable interest being the theme used by Sir Francis Bacon for his classic *The New Atlantis.*

I do not think Atlantis was in North America but if it was in the regions of Tarshish (Tartessos) there may be clues in Plato's story that it had ties with America for resources. In the following Atlantean passage 'headship' might mean at the head of the Mediterranean (Gibraltar) and exposed to the Americas: "For because of their headship, they a large supply of imports from abroad."

If the Atlanteans were at Tarshish they would know about North America through Poseidon, an extraterrestrial who would be aware of distant lands since according to *Timaeus* he was a member of gods that divided our world amongst themselves. Legends tell of Poseidon's son Atlas forming colonies in South America. And also we remember the symbols Professor Homet found in South America alluding to the Pleiades and the megalithic structures we think were left there by the Taurus giants. During the last century some Atlantists thought of the native Amerindian civilization as colonies of Atlantis. Perhaps there is some cold logic to it.

Ignatius T. T. Donnelly (1831–1901) was a man with an extremely active mind who must have acquired an enormous sheaf of notes for his book *Atlantis—The Antediluvian World.* He believed that the Atlantis account was not, as had long been supposed, fable, but veritable history, and that Atlantis was a region where man first rose from a state of barbarism to civilization and that civilization spread throughout the world. He believed that the ancient gods of the Mediterranean were real people, and on that point I agree at least as far as Poseidon is concerned and it is through Poseidon's cosmic influence that I believe some of Donnelly's theories are correct.

Donnelly was in a class by himself because he wrote an exhaustive work on the authenticity of Atlantis. Although it must be pointed out that after the Renaissance attempts were made to rationalize the account of Atlantis and in the seventeenth and eighteenth centuries the credibility of the legend was seriously debated, and sometimes admitted, even by Montaigne, Buffon and Voltaire.

There have been many approaches to the Atlantis account but few to my knowledge have dissected it word for word and studied it in the framework of the cosmic. The occultists quickly digested the story whole and expanded on it by psychic inspiration or literary flights of fancy. Academics have left out the supernatural elements, brought in wordy arguments and disclaimed the work as fiction. Some have taken the story as true but have erased or ignored the supernatural elements. To strike a balance we should put Atlantis in the framework Plato and probably the Egyptian priests intended it—the universe—the exact theme of *Timaeus* containing this work. It is in this framework of this new legitimate dimension that the supernatural and natural converge, revealing one day the truth of Atlantis. Perhaps we can even add perspective to this new dimension by keeping Plato away from it whenever we can. There has been too much confusion as to what Plato meant and did not mean pertaining to Atlantis. Plato meant nothing. He is only the courier of Atlantis whose only claim to it is his memorizing and wisdom to insert it in *Timaeus*. Actually it is Critias that is telling us the story. Whether or not Atlantis is true lies with the ancient Egyptian priests and beyond. With Plato removed, and penetrating our new line of focus beyond his time, it would not be wise to change the details of the account. Too often the story has been manipulated to suit aspects of Plato's life and work which has only brought confusion to the Egyptian narrative of Atlantis.

There are a lot of themes that resurge on Atlantism : the rise and sinking of land masses, the nature of myths, and the similarity of languages. But still, many doubt the existence of Atlantis and find it difficult to accept as unvarnished truth. Reasoning has been put forward that if you believe in the Atlantis myth pertaining to Poseidon then you should accept the other myths about him as well. If we make a beginning by accepting the Atlantis account as authentic I don't think it necessarily follows that we must accept all myths pertaining to Poseidon as factual, although we may be able to see mythology more clearly and understand such things as why Poseidon was a leading god in the Greek Pantheon or his mention in the *Odyssey*. However, I think for the most part mixing myths directly into Atlantis will distort the account further. Many mythology books, for example, are full of confusion and disagreement as to Poseidon's genealogy to other gods, and this approach to Atlantis will make it impossible to sort out the truth. Poseidon may not be the mortal king of an imaginary island with a complicated relationship to mythical gods as mythologists have stated. The truth of his existence may be basically simple—a celestial god as suggested in Atlantis.

During the last century North Africa drew considerable interest as a possible location for Atlantis. In 1868 Godron stated that Atlantis was in the Sahara. Felix Berlioux in 1874 claimed to have located the capital of Atlantis on the west coast of Morocco between Casablanca and Agadir, where the Atlas mountain chain tumbles down to the sea. It was in this region that Diodoros states was the city of Kerne, the capital of the Atlantoi. According to Dmitri Merejkowski in his book *Atlantis Europe*, 'Kerna' is a Greek derivative of the word 'horns' which may fit well with our Taurus bull theory. The convergence of the two names Agadir and Atlas into the region may have a connection with Poseidon's half celestial sons. Perhaps Morocco and nearby Tarshish were part of Atlantis or the Atlantis influence.

The eighteenth and nineteenth centuries were the halcyon days of the speculative atlantologists when many scholars felt inspired to construct exciting theories on the origins of mankind. Action-packed theories were presented by Buffon and Saint Vincent suggesting the swamping of Atlantis by earthquake waves and Carli had it exploded by a flaming comet.

Professor Leo Frobenius made a quieter study of the Atlantis question and concluded that there never was an island named Atlantis between Africa and the Americas. His studies convinced him that Atlantis was in Yorubaland in West Africa. In these regions he unearthed ruins of palaces and beautiful statuary. Compounding this, the Yorubans told him legends of an ancient royal city and its palace with golden walks which in time immemorial sank beneath the waves. If Atlantis was in Tarshish or North Africa it could have easily influenced these regions. Many of the researchers of Atlantis may not be finding its sources but its influence. Such an entity, particularly if it was cosmically inspired, would cast a vast reflection throughout the world, particularly in Africa, Europe and the Mediterranean, and this could be what explorers are coming in contact with even though the source could be generating from some smaller area such as Tarshish.

Colonel Alexandre Braghine, the French explorer, was convinced that the ancient Ethiopians were in some way connected with Atlantis. According to the Greek historian Proclus the Egyptian priests in Sais showed Kantor columns of hieroglyphs relating the history of Atlantis. Skylax of Karyanda mentioned in the last chapter recorded that Phoenician mariners carried on extensive trade with Ethiopians in the Island of Kerne, beyond the Pillars of Heracles in the Atlantic Ocean. Later Diodorus Siculus stated that the western region of Ethiopia was inhabited by Atlanteans. He also tells us that they bear the name of Autochthones which is the name of the youngest of Poseidon's third set of twins. He claims the Egyptians were colonists sent out by the Ethiopians, Osiris having been leader of the colony. Plato states Egypt was a colony of Atlantis and Osiris has been associated with the Egyptian Apis bull, like Poseidon a strong suggestion of his celestial origins in Taurus.

Perhaps in ancient times Ethiopia was not near its present

location. The name Ethiopia has been adopted in modern times by Abyssinia. Athiopes are first mentioned by Homer, who describes them as the furthest of mankind : "the gods go to their banquets and the sun probably sets in their country"—suggesting a western location. Homer mentions Poseidon being connected to this region.

Other areas associated with Atlantis have been the Isles of the Blest, or Fortunate Islands; Avalon; the Portuguese Antilla or Isle of Seven Cities; and St Brendan's Island, the subject of many sagas in many languages. All except Avalon were marked on maps of the fourteenth and fifteenth centuries and formed the object of voyages of discovery; conjecture as to the existence of St Brendan's Island persisted until the eighteenth century. Somewhat similar legends are those of the islands of the Phaecians (Homer, *Odyssey*), the Island of Brazil, of Lyonnesse (the sunken land off the Cornish coast), of the lost Breton city of Is, and of Mayda or Asmaide, the French Ile Verte and Portuguese Ilha Verde or Green Island.

We learn from L. Sprague de Camp's *Lost Continents, The Atlantis Theme* that interesting theories have been put forward pertaining to the location of Atlantis—even the bottom of the Mediterranean! :

Others such as the naturalist Buffon, a contemporary of Saint-Vincent, thought that Atlantis had been washed away by water flowing in the opposite direction, from the Atlantic into the Mediterranean, which theretofore had been mostly dry land. Modern geology tends to support this view. During the last advance of Pleistocene ice, say some geologists, the Mediterranean was a great low plain with a pair of large lakes separated by the ridge connecting Italy and Sicily with Africa. During the warm interglacial periods apelike men hunted pigmy elephants and hippopotami in Sicily. With the final melting of the ice-caps the ocean rose until, about 15,000 years ago, it broke through the Isthmus of Gibraltar and filled the Mediterranean basin to its present level, forcing thousands of men and millions of animals to flee. A catastrophe? The origin of Plato's story, with the Mediterranean Valley playing the role of Atlantis? Suggested but not proved.

Perhaps in the future Atlantis will be found once and for all. Perhaps in ancient Tarshish with its Taurus-sounding name or nearby Morocco. It may be that from this vantage point it influenced many regions including the neighbourhood of the seven stars—the Mediterranean.

# SEVEN

# Atlantis and Anthropology

OUR RECORDED HISTORY is recent and presents an orderly sequence of evolution of mankind on this planet. But it may well be in the smoky mists of prehistory that the secrets of our anthropological evolution lie, holding secrets much more exciting than conventional anthropology. I think anthropology could be further aided if anthropologists paid more attention to ancient literature as well as archaeological finds – literature such as Atlantis and apocryphal texts that have been taken as myths. This literature may in fact be anthropological records of earthmen and giants from space.

Using the tools of human biology, archaeology and the study of living cultures, particularly those of primitive men, anthropologists have had good success tracing the evolution of mankind on this planet—the group represented by Cleito and Evenor in Atlantis. It is the arrival of Poseidon and the giants from space that is missing from anthropology even though megalithic structures and giant bones have been found around the world.

There seems to be a gap in our anthropological story that does not correlate with our ancient literature. Anthropology takes us up to and beyond, but not including the mating of Poseidon from space with Cleito, the other mating of giants with earth women in the Book of Enoch, and the mating of the Sons of God with earth women in the Bible.

There was no doubt some order and assembly amongst earth people before the extraterrestrial intervention. Anthropology has

56

many records of various cultures on this planet since men first formed groups.

As earthmen progessively conquered the forces of nature, more and more people were no doubt brought into contact and primitive societies arose, containing the family, band, council, leadership, etc. However it appears that the complex institutions that arose from these primitive structures came too fast, particularly in the areas of the Mediterranean. The development of such things as manufacturing, trading, shipping, etc., may have been speeded along by cosmic intervention.

It may have been the arrival of Poseidon from space who initiated the Mediterranean regions of our planet that caused us to reach this point of climax. Whatever your views, the story of man, being unique and dramatic, is well worth the speculation.

There are three key points to be considered in our space theories of the Atlantis story, all of which have a great bearing on the field of anthropology: 1. Cleito and Evenor are part of orthodox evolution as we know it in our world; 2. Poseidon is of a group of humanoids in space; 3. Poseidon's sons because of the highly unusual circumstance of being five sets of twins and all male were probably, scientifically, genetically programmed in a superior fashion to initiate the pioneering of Poseidon's newly acquired planet.

To what extent Cleito's group advanced before the arrival of Poseidon is not clear. Her group probably acquired the basic habits of dealing with one another which still guide the behaviour of individuals, communities and nations. But it was probably on the arrival of Poseidon that her group suddenly built chariots, smelted copper, invented writing, and embarked on a rapid sequence of social advances that moved swiftly to horses, iron, money, deep-water ships, and the glittering palaces we see in Atlantis. We are reminded again of the key phrase in Atlantis that shipping was not in existence in our world until the arrival of Poseidon. Unless there were other interventions from space in prehistory we can conclude that Cleito is an original product of our planet—which raises exciting questions as to whether man originates separately in remote regions of the universe or if all have a common origin at some unknown point. It is interesting to note that the Greek word for the branch is *clado*, perhaps from Cleito because in effect that is what Poseidon and Cleito were—separate branches of evolutionary chains.

Although Cleito's ancestor's bones are scarce, the product of their handiwork is abundant through the finds of anthropology and archaeology. Certain literature such as the Bible, Enoch, Atlantis and Homer may shed further light on Cleito.

We may have in the poetry of Homer a priceless document of an early civilization transplanted to the Mediterranean *region* from Atlantis. Whatever classical scholars have to say about the period depicted, the date of the composition of the epics, or even of Homer himself or the uncertain authorship of these works, two points are worthy of consideration : the culture depicted may be a whole culture and a real one because it makes sense internally. It is doubtful that Homer created such a vast civilization out of fantasy. The Homeric civilization could be essentially that of an early reflection of the Atlantis island lying near Gibraltar that spread its influence throughout the entire Mediterranean area.

The setting seems to be in a land richer in nature than that of today. Dark evergreens towered over serene meadows surrounded by sculptured mountains. Lions, leopards and wild boar roamed the woods, along with bear, deer and fox, while perennial springs supplied water to men and animals.

Through Homer's epic we may be seeing the resulting influence of Atlantis bringing earthmen out of the dark ages. The carpenters built houses, ships and chariots, while the smiths made weapons, tools and armour. Anthropology had been altered on our planet but Poseidon's plan for social development was now well in the stages of being carried out.

# EIGHT

# The Taurus Bull

SOME WRITERS believe that it is probable that: the form of
the bull and the bull's proclivities were assigned to the Taurus
constellation, because the bull was used by the ancients to plow
fields, and the season set aside for plowing and furrowing
corresponded to the time in which the sun reached the segment
of the heavens named Taurus.

I think we emphasize primitive conditions on earth too much
in order to explain cosmic connotations. The constellation was
introduced on Earth by Poseidon and other celestials. The bull
became deified as a sign from heaven and the gods to mortal men
on Earth—a phenomenon that was carried on until our historians
found it permeating the entire ancient world of our recorded
history. In fact, remnants are probably still in evidence today in
India in accordance with the worship of sacred bulls in esoteric
religions.

Apart from the bull ceremony taking place in Plato's Atlantis,
the earliest written record we probably have of an individual
making use of the bull symbol is in connection with the famous
maps copied by the Turkish admiral Piri Reis in 1513 and 1528.
They show mountains in an ice-free Antarctic and two broad
gulfs in Queen Maud Land. Equally striking, Greenland consists
of three islands, later confirmed by present-day oceanographers.
It has been suggested that the original maps were possibly drawn
before the ice age in 10,000 B.C. from aerial surveys—a similar
method believed to have been used by celestials in locating the
Great Pyramid in the centre of the world's land mass.

There was a notation by Piri Reis that in compiling his map he had used old charts and world maps drawn in the days of Alexander, 'Lord of the Two Horns', which show an inhabited quarter of the world. Through his superior methods of aerial photography we might infer that Alexander himself was a Pleiades celestial emblazing his sign of the Taurus bull's two horns on Earth. We wonder further to what extent he may be connected to Poseidon and the original group that divided up our world.

The bull occupied an outstanding position in the cultures of the early Mediterranean. The figure eight often accompanied the bull which is probably a sign of the universe denoting infinity. The Rig-Veda (the oldest literature in the world) describes Dyaus as a reddish bull, roaring downwards, suggesting a cosmic strategy.

The Gilgamesh Epic in Babylonian scripture mentions that King Gilgamesh is "two thirds god and one third human". This could be a reflection of the Pleiades union with earth people mentioned earlier. Throughout the tale there is allegory pertaining to the Bull of Heaven. His friend Enkidu is referred to as half bull and half man; a purely mythical creature, or, more profoundly, a descendant of the Earth and the Pleiades and genetically similar to Atlas and his brothers on Atlantis. Gilgamesh is tempted by Ishtar whom he rejects, so the outraged goddess sends down a bull from heaven to devastate Erech; the bull is eventually slain by Gilgamesh. Perhaps the bull presented here is a Pleiades celestial.

Meroach or Marduk was a deified celestial of Babylon and known as 'the Bull of Light'. The Creation Epic gives a description of his luminous appearance and technological advancements often associated with celestials—"his body filled with blazing fire, he set the lightning in front of him, he rode the storm chariot". His activities were associated with the war between the Spirits of Light and the Powers of Evil, similar to the conflict in Egypt between Horus and Set.

In Canaan religion Baal is mentioned as a god who takes on the symbol of a bull. He is mentioned as Baal the mighty and "he who mounts the clouds". He dwelt on the summit of the city of Ras Shamra.

The Minotaur (half man and half bull), so often associated with the legends of Crete, may be a distorted version over thousands of years stemming from people like Poseidon's sons who were half celestial (cosmic bull) and half Earth born. In the sanctuaries of Crete there are horns of clay, stones and authentic horns, found on the roofs and on the altars. The Greek word for horns is so immemorially ancient its origins may lie in Atlantis or the cosmic. The capital of Atlantis according to Diodorus was 'Kerna' a derivative of the Greek 'Kerata'. This root can be traced through Crete and may come from the original name 'Knossos', 'Kairatos', 'Kaaeratos'. There is also the 'cosmic' island itself, Kretes. Cretan settlers in Canaan were men of the horned god bull or the 'Kheretim'.

The sacred horns of Crete probably signify the deification of the cosmic bull, and may correlate to the two-horned moon found in pile buildings in Switzerland, Lower Austria, Savoy, Hungary and Italy, believed to have originated from the beginnings of the Bronze and Iron Ages.

The divine horns of the lamb are recorded in the Apocalypse:
"In the midst of the throne . . . stood a lamb as it had been slain, having seven horns."

Our constant study of the universe will reveal that these immemorially ancient symbols signify inter-galactic messages.

Even as recently as two hundred years ago it was customary for the natives on the Island of Inis Marce, Scotland, to sacrifice a bull on 25 August to the god Mowrie and his devilans. The Scottish name for a bull is 'bill', possibly a corruption of 'Bel'. The palenque cross has been found on the head of bulls and we are reminded of the blood running down the Taurus inscriptions from the slain sacrificial bull on Atlantis.

Similar to Atlantis, the Druidical rite of Beltane's Fire sacrificed bulls. Lewis Spence asserts that the legends and traditions of the Celtic people consist of a substratum of Druid-Atlantean religion with a layer of later Celtic beliefs imposed on them.

Michelangelo associated the cosmic bull with Moses. His well-known carving entitled 'Moses' showed an imaginary veil of the bull's mask with two ray horns—a strong suggestion that the famous law-giver was in touch with great dimensions of the universe. The sons and daughters of Israel worshipped the molten calf Jahwe in the Sinai desert, a corruption probably of the Taurus bull. A double of a Cretan bull is shown goring a warrior on an Egyptian quartz tablet, and we are reminded of the Assyro–Babylon winged bull cherub. There is a Yucatan–Palenque cross on the head of a bull, Minotaur, and little clay idols of the glacial god bull, Bison, have been found in the Tuc d'Audebert cave. The bull is depicted on the golden carved goblets from Vaphio in Laconia and some think they are precisely similar to the chase of the sacrificial bull of the ten kings of Atlantis. The accumulation of these facts may be inescapable evidence that the cosmic bull from Taurus exists on our planet as the most gigantic, most universal and eternal symbol hieroglyph ever given to earthmen from the universe.

The remnants of this Taurus influence may still be in existence today in India. In the Hindu Trinity the bull is sacred to Shiva, the god of destruction. In this most fascinating of all countries that cloaks many secrets of man and his universe, the freedom and privileges of the Brahman bull are inviolate. Even when it is destructive the bull must not be restrained. In India we may be seeing a preservation of Poseidon's cult when sacred bulls roamed freely on Atlantis representing heaven and earth.

It may be that the cow received preferential treatment in this ancient country only because it was associated with an earthly bull that happened to be a cosmic symbol. There is evidence that cows were not always sacred in India, and used as articles of food. The Atharva-Veda chastises 'cow killing' as the most horrific of crimes, and capital punishment was inflicted on anyone who harmed a cow in any way. Even the cow's urine and dung are sacred to the Brahmans.

The most important of all symbolic animals was the Apis, or Egyptian bull of Memphis, which is said to be the sacred vehicle for the transmigration of the soul of the god Osiris. One version states that the Apis was conceived by a bolt or lightning, and the ceremony attendant upon its selection and consecration was one of the most impressive in Egyptian ritualism. Osiris was probably a contemporary of Poseidon who was among the gods in *Timaeus* that divided the world. Like Poseidon he took the bull as the symbol of his origins—the Taurus constellation.

It was important to mark the Apis very accurately. Ancient writers state that the sacred bull was marked with twenty-nine symbols, his body was spotted and his right side was painted with the form of a crescent. After his sanctification the Apis was kept in a stable adjacent to the temple. He was led in processions through the streets of the city upon solemn occasions.

"The worship of the bull was not confined to Egypt and India but was prevalent in many nations of the ancient world. The Persians and Jews regarded the bull as an important religious symbol. The Assyrians, Phoenicians, Chaldeans, and Greeks reverenced this animal. At his death the bull was frequently mummified and buried with the full rights of a god. Excavations at the Serapeum at Memphis have uncovered the tombs of more than sixty of these sacred animals." The origins of all this are in Plato's Atlantis which contains our first record of the bull being introduced on this planet as a sacred symbol of the Taurus constellation.

How pervasive and extensive the Taurus symbol was on earth still remains to be discovered. It may have appeared more dramatically than we can comprehend. According to Velikovsky many races on earth have legends of the planet Venus suddenly appearing in our solar system. And when it appeared its comet smoke formed horns and gave the appearance of a bull. The planet Venus may have been pushed out of the Pleiades and ridden to earth by Taurus celestials; locking into the orbit of our solar system they displayed their arrival to us with the Taurus symbol.

Having said this, I'm not sure whether or not I believe it. However, one thing I am convinced of, if the Pleiades celestials were on earth they would certainly be familiar with the other planets in our solar system, since they would have to pass by most of them on their arrival to Earth.

Ancient legends usually ascribe gods as coming from nearby planets in our solar system. For example, South American legends strongly associate Virachocha and Quetzalcoatl with Venus. This may mean that the Pleiades celestials were on our nearby planets as well as our own. After travelling 400 light years to our solar system Earth would not be their only interest. Further exploration of our neighbouring planets may reveal clues they left on their cosmic trails.

We would gain a great deal in our overall view of mankind if we could establish the history of the major changes of our civilization. The island of Atlantis, the biblical flood and the sudden appearance of the planet Venus in our solar system may all be true events that played a significant role in our evolution on this planet. These events could have taken place through the initiation of Pleiades celestials who have left us signs everywhere to see like the cosmic bull from Taurus.

# NINE

# The Taurus Giants

SOME CONTEMPORARY religious leaders have denounced the Book of Enoch as fiction and there do seem to be passages of a questionable nature, particularly those with unbelievable geographical indications and incredibly large numbers used for descriptive purposes. There are also spiritual descriptions that are beyond our limitations to grasp. Still, the Book of Enoch belongs in our treasury of literature and scattered throughout its passages may be authentic history.

Actually, the Book of Enoch may be the oldest and most valuable book in the world. There is much speculation as to its antiquity, and even its foremost authority, Bruce, was uncertain as to its age. Some scholars speculate that it is the world's most authentic bible. It may directly stem from the Book of Noah which may have been the first book given to mankind on Earth by celestials.

Most writers of the New Testament were aware of the Book of Enoch and seemed to be influenced by it. In Genesis 5 v. 18–24 and Luke 3 v. 37, Enoch is claimed to be the father of Methuselah and to have been associated with God. Among the world's earlier clerics it was considered to have all the power of profound scripture.

We almost lost it when it passed out of circulation and disappeared from the Western world. This came about from the fourth century onward when the book suffered discredit and was banned by leaders such as Hilary, Jerome and Augustine. It would have been lost in the annals of time if it were not for

Bruce who found an Ethiopic version of the work over a century ago in Abyssinia and returned to his native Scotland with three manuscripts of it. Laurence made the first modern translation of his find.

This complex book contains a large variety of religious forms and at times runs parallel to the Bible. However, one thought is repeated several times throughout its passages : giants (presumably from outer space) had intercourse with earth women, siring giants. The new breed of giants eventually became degenerate and corrupt to the point where certain powers in the heavens deemed it necessary to destroy the Earth in a flood so that mankind on Earth could start over again. Perhaps the general theme of the Atlantis account and in compliance with our theories of giants such as Poseidon arriving on earth from the Pleiades.

Parts of the book such as the following passage are in allegory and others are straightforward :

LXXXVI 1. "And again I saw with mine eyes as I slept, and I saw the heaven above, and behold a star fell from heaven, and it arose and eat and pastured amongst those oxen."
2. "And after that I saw the large black oxen, and behold they all changed their stalls and pastures and their cattle, and began to live with each other."
3. "And again I saw in the vision, and looked towards heaven, and behold I saw many stars descend and cast themselves down from heaven to that first star, and they became bulls amongst those cattle and pastured with them (amongst them)."
4. "And I looked at them and saw, and behold they all let out their privy members, like horses, and began to cover the cows of the oxen, and they all became pregnant and bare elephants, camels and asses.'
5. "And all the oxen feared them and were affrighted at them, and began to bite with their teeth and to devour, and to gore with their horns."
6. "And they began moreover to devour these oxen; and behold all the children of the earth began to tremble and quake before them and to flee from them."

The passages just quoted might be interpreted this way—
1. Star = spaceship. It lands on the Earth and mixes with the earth people (oxen).

2. The earth people reorganize their society probably under the guidance of the initiators from space.

3. More spaceships descend and join the first ship that has already landed. Bulls are the celestials from Taurus and they mix with the earth people.

4. Through this mixing they relax their ranks and have intercourse with the earth women (cows): The women become pregnant and give birth to three kinds of giants (elephants, camels, asses).

5. And all the earth people fear them and try to fight back, using whatever weaponry they have.

6. The giants get the upper hand and begin to devour the earth people.

If the following Enoch passages are not myth they may be one of the most powerful clues of the Taurus giants being on Earth. We notice the descent of the celestials on Mount Hermon, perhaps a strong clue they landed from space. The description of earth women mating with angels (celestials) is similar to the Bible. It also agrees with our theories of Poseidon and Cleito and their 'star-trek' romance ordained in the heavens.

These passages are most thought-provoking from an anthropological and sociological point of view. In fact, if they are mostly true, one could reflect upon them endlessly, particularly on such passages as earthmen learning writing and war. This particular entity was a destructive group on Earth probably from space.

Enoch states:

VI "And it came to pass when the children of men had multiplied that in those days were born unto them beautiful and comely daughters. And the angels, the children of the heaven, saw and lusted after them, and said to one another: 'Come, let us choose us wives from among the children of men and beget us children'."

3. "And Semjaza who was their leader, said unto them: 'I fear ye will not indeed agree to do this deed, and I alone shall have to pay the penalty of a great sin'."

4. "And they all answered him and said: 'Let us all swear an oath, and all bind ourselves by mutual imprecations not to abandon this plan but to do this thing.' "

5. "Then sware they all together and bound themselves by mutual imprecations upon it."

6. "And they were in all two hundred; who descended in the days of Jared on the summit of Mount Hermon, and they called it Mount Hermon because they had sworn and bound themselves by mutual imprecations upon it."

7. "And these are the names of their leaders: Semiazaz, Danel, Ezeqeel, Baraqijal, Asael, Armaros, Batarel, Ananel, Zaqiel, Samsapeel, Satarel, Turel, Jomael, Sariel."

8. "These are their chiefs of tens."

VII 1. "And all the others together with them took unto themselves wives, and each chose for himself one, and they began to go in unto them and to defile themselves with them, and they taught them charms and enchantments, and the cutting of roots, and made them acquainted with plants."

2. "And they became pregnant, and they bare great giants, whose height was three thousand ells."

3. "Who consumed all the acquisitions of men. And when men could no longer sustain them,"

4. "The giants turned against them and devoured mankind."

5. "And they began to sin against birds, and beasts, and reptiles, and fish, and to devour one another's flesh and drink the blood."

6. "Then the earth laid accusation against the lawless ones."

VIII 1. "And Azazel taught men to make swords, and knives and shields, and breastplates, and made known to them the metals (of the earth) and the art of working them, and bracelets, and ornaments, and the use of antimony, and the beautifying of the eyelids, and all kinds of costly stones, and all colouring tinctures."

2. "And there arose much godlessness, and they committed fornication, and they were led astray, and became corrupt in all their ways."

3. "Semjaza taught enchantments, and root-cuttings, Armaros the resolving of enchantments, Baraqijal (taught) astrology, Kokabel the constellations."

4. "The name of the first Jeqon: that is the one who led astray (all) the sons of God, and brought them astray through the daughters of men."

5. "And the second was named Asbeel: he imparted to the holy sons of God evil counsel, and led them astray so that they defiled their bodies with the daughters of men."

6. "And the third was named Gadreel: he is who showed the children of men all the blows of death, and he led astray Eve, and showed (the weapons of death to the sons of men) the shield and the

coat of mail, and the sword for battle, and all the weapons of death to the children of men."

7. "And from his hand they have proceeded against those who dwell on the earth from that day and for evermore."

8. "And the fourth was named Penemue : he taught them all the secrets of their wisdom."

9. "And he instructed mankind in writing with ink and paper, and thereby many sinned from eternity and until this day."

10. "For men were not created for such a purpose, to give confirmation to their good faith with pen and ink."

11. "For men were created exactly like the angels, to the intent that they should continue pure and righteous, and death, which destroys everything, could not have taken hold of them, but through this power it is consuming me."

12. "And the fifth was named Kasdeja : this is he who showed the children of men all the wicked smitings of spirits and demons, and the smitings of the embryo in the womb, that it may pass away."

Possibly, these events were going on simultaneously around the world at the time of Atlantis. I suspect much of the evil mentioned here is parallel with the last degenerate days of Atlantis recited by Plato.

*TEN*

# The Taurus Empire

THE MYSTERIOUS REGIONS of Malta like Crete may be another 'cosmic island' that conceals great universal truths in its megalithic remains. The titanic monuments suggest the dwelling place of giants, and there are innumerable tunnels with three-storey underground chambers and wells that descend into the earth, the purpose of which is not known. There are also mysterious tracks that lead out to the sea, inferring that Malta must once have been larger than it is now, and connected with the nearby islands of Gozo, Comino and Filfa—to Italy or Africa.

The German geologist Hoffman, as well as other scientists, have stated that in geologically recent times the entire regions of North Africa lay submerged underneath the Mediterranean, and what are now its mountains and plateaux formed great islands. The suggestion was made long ago by Albert Mayr, Sir Arthur Evans and other archaeologists that there was a cultural connection between Crete and Malta.

The tracks are from three and a half to five inches wide and are very ancient, underlying tombs of the Phoenician period and deposits that date back further still. The lower part of a female statue found at Hal Tarxien, suggests the dwelling place of giants, yet the stone implements that have been discovered are of normal size. Perhaps they belong to a later era when the Taurus giants had been destroyed or returned to space. The stone implements cannot explain the engineering and scale of the Maltese structures, and there is a complete absence of metal tools on the island.

70

Several edifices contain rectangular stone blocks almost twelve feet square, surrounded by walls on three sides and bordered by a stone step.

Another mystery is the appearance in Malta of the spiral design which, in many parts of this planet, signifies our galaxy. It corresponds to the actual configuration of our galaxy in space. This helps to strengthen our case for Taurus giants being on earth.

Another symbol found is the Tau Cross. It closely resembles the letter T. It is suspected that this symbol originated amongst the Egyptians from the spread of the horns of a bull and the vertical lines of the face. It probably existed before the Egyptians as a symbol used by the Taurus giants. The Tau appears to be the oldest form of the cross extant and was probably introduced into the world by beings such as Osiris and Poseidon.

The Tau Cross was inscribed on the forehead of every person admitted into the mysteries of Mithras. When a king was admitted into the Egyptian mysteries, the Tau was placed against his lips, perhaps symbolizing a linkage of himself to the Taurus constellation. It was tattooed on the bodies of the candidates in some of the American Indian mysteries. To the Qabbalist the Tau meant heaven. An oak tree, cut and assembled in this form, was the symbol of the Druid god Hu. The biblical prophet Ezekiel states that the Tau Cross was the sign which the Lord told the people of Jerusalem to make upon their foreheads.

Manly P. Hall in *The Secret Teachings of All Ages* states: "In one of the Qabbalistic Masonic legends, Chiram Abiff is given a hammer in the form of a Tau by his ancestor, Tubal Cain. The Tau cross is preserved to modern masonry under the symbol of the T square." Perhaps these are clues that the origins of Masonry lie somewhere in the constellation of Taurus.

Mediterranean tradition said the Greek gods were based among other places in Italy, Sicily and North Africa. The classical Greeks placed Atlas on the majestic mountains of north-west Africa and the Canary Islands, with civilizations on both sides of the Mediterranean. Associated with Atlas were other giants usually referred to as Titans.

Lixus, its huge cyclopean walls still towering, the city of the sun, was the Moroccan harbour from which much of the Atlantic trade commenced. This could have been one of the principal cities of Atlantis from where the descendants of Taurus sent forth their empire of the sun around the world.

Certainly the Ashanti retain a great many traces of this ancient world, perhaps because their name sounds like Atlantis and they are descendants of the Atlantean Empire. A chief is called Nana, resembling the Sumerian word for god or king. There are Ashanti bronzes that are Mediterranean rather than African in style. The Ekuaba figures resemble the cycladic idols of the third millennium B.C. An Ashanti, J. B. Danquah, declared that an Ashanti national symbol was a kingfisher or halcyon and that Alcyon was a daughter of Atlas. Another daughter was Maia, a colony on the other side of the Atlantic in Guatemala. Hesiod refers to her as Atlantis Maia. Two of the Pleiades stars are connected in name to these daughters which makes us wonder further about the connection between Atlantis, the North African regions and the Pleiades.

African legends help to substantiate the dwelling place of Atlas in Africa who was probably a giant like his father Poseidon. These legends tell of giants who were marvellous men with shining eyes and unbreakable courage who opened up unknown country. One should not look them in the face, the legend adds, because of the brightness of their eyes. There are other references such as this to shining eyes in ancient scripture usually when celestials are suspected. This could refer to artificial devices around the eyes to accustom them to a new planet or the natural state of their own native planet and not ours.

Actual remains of giants have been found in Africa by Richard Leakey. Giant hominid remains were accidentally discovered when he was scaling the precarious cliffs of Olduvai Gorge, near Lake Victoria. Suddenly he spotted a large bone protruding from the soil causing him in his anxiety to slip and nearly lose his balance. Digging it frantically out of the ground he found it to be a huge jawbone, with teeth as big as a human finger. Human skeletons ranging from 11 to 17 feet have been found in other parts of the world.

It seems that the giants existed. It may indeed be that the giants came from extraterrestrial space, and as my evidence attempts to show, from the constellation of Taurus. It appears there are many mysterious traces of the Earth's remote past which seem to support the hypothesis of interplanetary links with that particular constellation.

The port of Calabar may contain further evidence of the Taurus Atlantean Empire. There are many monoliths engraved with Mediterranean Bronze Age symbols—the Maltese Cross on the monolith outside the front of the Lagos museum, the spiral signifying our galaxy, and the sun circles often associated with Atlantis.

That the Taurus Empire circled the world may be in evidence in South America. The huge blocks of stone at Tiahuanaco were held together by copper and sometimes gold rivets, a method of building construction found also in Assyria and Etruria. Some blocks of stone used at Tiahuanaco weighed 100 and others even 200 tons. These were brought from Kiappa, a distance of 40 miles. The walls at Tiahuanaco are double paralleled with large stones outside and the centre filled with soil—a method of building used in the 'cosmic island' of Crete and, indeed, all over the Middle East. Megalithic structures are scattered all over the world.

There is a legend of Poseidon's son, the half-celestial Atlas, a nation of white Africans and Mediterranean men akin to the Berbers locating the Atlas dynasty in the white highlands of Bolivia and across the expanse of America to include Mexico. Some scholars identify him with the great cultural hero of Mexico and South America, Quetzalcoatl, and suggest that this giant Atlas carries a name that became Mexican and old Mediterranean Atl, meaning sea dwellers in both instances.

The sun symbol is on many megalithic structures around the world and Manly P. Hall states :

Atlantean sun worship has been perpetuated in the ritualism and ceremonialism of both christianity and pagandom. Both the cross and the serpent were Atlantean emblems of divine wisdom. The divine (Atlantean) progenitors of the Mayas and Qhichas of Central America coexisted within the green and azure radiance of Gucamatz, the 'plumed serpent'. The six sky born sages came into manifestation as centres of light bound together synthesised by the seventh—and chief of their order, the 'feathered snake'. (see Popul Vuh). The title of 'winged' or 'plumed' snake was applied to Quetzalcoatl or Kukulcan, the central American initiate. The centre of the Atlantean wisdom religion was presumably a great pyramidal temple standing on the brow of a plateau rising in the midst of the city with the golden gates. From here the initiate priests of the Sacred Feather went forth carrying the keys of universal wisdom to the uttermost parts of the world.

Various names may apply to the basic Atlantis theme such as Atlas being Quetzalcoatl. The Phaecians for example may be only another name for the Atlanteans. The royal line of the Phaecians is ascribed as descended from the god Poseidon. They appear to have lived in the neighbourhood of Tartessos which in another chapter we state may have been Atlantis or part of it. They describe themselves in the *Odyssey*: "Though our boxing and wrestling are not beyond criticism we can run fast and we are first rate seamen. But the things that we take a perennial delight in are the feast, the lyre, the dance, clean linen in plenty, a hot bath and our beds."

Thucydides, in the introduction to his history, says that Minos of Crete was the first to whom tradition ascribes the possession of a navy. Ships and sailing were not in existence until Poseidon arrived from space and this may have come about through his influence. Living by its sea trade Ancient Crete probably played a great part in the Taurus Atlantean Empire. Ancient Crete probably traded with Atlantis, Egypt and Tuscany. To the Greek Cretans, the celestial Poseidon was a very important deity. And if this Taurus giant and his descendants influenced an Atlantean empire around the world we are led to the speculation of how such a regime was ruled.

The clues to this may lie in Plato's *Republic* which was probably cosmically influenced like his Atlantis account. The *Republic*, like Atlantis, is another work that has been credited as belonging only to the imagination of Plato. It may be worthy of consideration that the *Republic* is not an imaginative creation of an ideal state as scholars have believed. It may be a historical description underlying the casualness of conversational dialectic, of how the Pleiades giants ruled Atlantis, the Mediterranean and the rest of the world.

The ideal state of the *Republic* may have been born in the Pleiades and brought to earth where it existed in the world's early societies, and hence this is how Plato eventually came by it, through his travels and studies as a young man. At times Plato seems too brilliant amongst earth mortals. He must have drawn much of his knowledge from other sources than himself.

# ELEVEN

# The Taurus Giants in South America

THE RELIGIOUS LEGENDS of the pre-Inca peoples state that the universe was inhabited by 'gods' and celestials arrived on Earth from the Pleiades. Other legends in the world tell of 'gods' that sailed the oceans of space in fireships and touched Earth as a port of call, initiating new civilizations on our planet in the process.

In South America there stands a place that appears to be the landing area of giants from space. Near Lake Titicaca, in Bolivia, stand the immense remains of Tiahuanaco, perhaps the oldest city on Earth. It stands at 12,300 feet above sea level, which suggests a suitability only for space ships. The age of this strange city is not known. The Incas had no idea and aptly called the mysterious ruins Tiahuanaco, the Place of the Dead. The Aymaras told the Spanish historiographer Cieza de Leon, one of the earliest European explorers in 1549, that the city was built by bearded white men and raised in a night. The Peruvians acknowledged the unknown city to be of even older date than that acknowledged by the Incas and that no one had seen the city for Tiahuanaco had been built in the night of mankind.

The macroscopic ruins of Tiahuanaco may stand now as a monument to giantry. All the buildings still show impressive grandeur in size and conception. The fortress of Akapana, a large truncated pyramid, towers 170 feet in height from a base about 650 by 600 feet. The Temple of the Sun, the Kalasasaya, measures about 440 by 390 feet and the Place of Sarcophagi 220 by 180 feet; the ruins of Tuncu Puncu or Place of Ten Doors form an artificial mound about 50 feet in height and 200 feet square. Such cyclopean structures would present problems even for technicians today; many huge slabs measure 36 by 7 feet and weigh 200 tons. It should be worthy of consideration that such structures, combined with Inca legends of gods from the Pleiades, were built by Taurus giants.

The Egyptians transported their obelisk from Aswan, the mysterious builders of Stonehenge brought their stone blocks from south-west Wales and Marlborough, the unknown sculptors of Easter Island took the material for their weird monster statues from a distant quarry to their present sites, but no one can say where some of the monoliths at Tiahuanaco come from. Perhaps they were brought in on convoys from space. It would be more efficient and practical for spacemen to bring in prefabricated structures to a new planet for immediate shelter than waiting unprotected after landing until an unknown quarry was discovered and worked.

Today, the city of Tiahuanaco is cloaked in secrecy. Commencing from Cuzco, Peru, the city and excavation sites are reached after several days' travel by rail and boat. The area has an interstellar eeriness, reminding one of the terrain of an unknown planet. Manual labour is exhausting for anyone who is not a native. The atmospheric pressure is about half as low as it is at sea level and the oxygen content of the air is correspondingly small.

The fact that an enormous city stood here makes us wonder if the giants had artificial breathing devices when they landed from space, or if the light air was automatically suitable to them without such aids. Such imaginative speculation is legitimate because there are no authentic traditions about Tiahuanaco. This can free us from orthodox learning and allow us to speculate in the realm of the imagination where the true answer may lie. Over the immemorially ancient ruins lies the mist of the past, ignorance and mystery. These old ruins may hold many secrets of the giants and the Taurus constellation.

Blocks of sandstone weighing 100 tons were covered with other

60-ton blocks for walls. Smooth surfaces with extremely accurate chamfers join enormous squared stones which are held together with copper clamps. In addition all the stonework is exceptionally neatly executed. Holes 8 feet long, whose purpose has not been explained thus far, are found in blocks weighing 10 tons. The $16\frac{1}{2}$-foot long, worn-down flagstones cut out of the one piece do not contribute to the solution of the mystery that Tiahuanaco conceals. Stone conduits 6 feet long and $1\frac{1}{2}$ feet wide are found scattered on the ground, possibly left by a huge catastrophe of some sort.

Sascahuaman shocks our credibility even more, making it difficult for us to conceive what technology was used to extract a colossal rock of more than 100 tons from a quarry and then transport it and work it in a distant location. Near the fortifications of Sascahuaman is a block that weighs 20,000 tons, the size of a four-storey building. It has signs of being crafted with steps and ramps and is ornamented with spirals and holes. It seems more plausible that this stone block was fashioned by the superior forces of the Taurus giants than by the obviously limited Incas.

In 1940, Professor Marcel Homet, the archaeologist now living in Stuttgart and author of the well-known book *Sons of the Sun*, discovered a giant stone egg 328 feet long and 98 feet high on the upper Rio Branco in North Amazonas, Brazil. On this colossal block, which was called Piedra Pintada, or painted stone, Homet found countless letters, crosses and sun symbols over a surface area of some 700 square yards.

In the Amazon, and above all in the Chulin Grotto in Argentina, Professor Homet found the most important inscription of all—'the bull head'. It is our theory that the Pleiades space giants took above all else as their symbol the sign of the bull, based on their zodiac sign of Taurus the Bull. It is highly possible they are the very ones who gave us the zodiac sign. They could have started mapping our skies shortly after their arrival on earth, dividing the sky into twelve parts and inscribing Taurus the Bull as the first sign designated. This is based on the fact that no one knows the origin of the zodiac and the ancient astronomer priests

attributed all their knowledge of it to celestials. The bull symbol
representing Taurus and the Pleiades might be likened to a flag
projected in the heavens and wherever that symbol is found is
representative of their domain. In the same way the American
flag transplanted around the world is representative of the U.S.
and put there by Americans, the people from Taurus placed the
symbol of the bull when they conquered Earth. Other planets
in our galaxy may be 'stamped' in the same way.

Professor Homet makes another exciting discovery on a disc
that seems to show the Pleiades group suggesting the setting up of
a theocratic government to the natives. The bulls could be symbolic of Pleiades spacemen. The Cretan axes may be symbolic
of pioneering a new world :

> Then there are two priests who are presented just like those in
> the Chulin Grotto of Argentina, where they appear surrounded
> by bulls and Cretan axes. On this disc they suggest the erection of
> a theocratic government. This will be founded on a study of the
> 'heavens' which is shown here by a circle with seven dots; it is
> the 'circle with the seven stars' which has been retained in the
> Amazonian legend of Ceuci; it is the constellation of the Pleiades,
> of the Cabiri and consequently of the Deity himself.

This is in keeping with the Inca legends of giants descending
from the clouds and having sexual intercourse with Incan women.
There are similar myths in almost every culture. These stories
create a profound case for visitations from other planets. Greek
mythology relates that gods and goddesses descended from the
skies and lived with mortals. The North American Indians have
tales of white beings who came down out of the skies and helped
them during times of crisis. Ancient legends report that beings
from the skies landed on Earth. These people were of exceptional
stature and marvellous beauty, and were gifted with transcendent
wisdom.

However, like all great civilizations they flourished and then
gradually went into decay. There is an ancient legend pertaining
to the giants in South America which corresponds to the Book
of Enoch. According to the Book of Enoch the giants went into

decay on Earth after mixing with earth people. This produced an inferior giant that ravaged the Earth. Nature corrected itself by a cosmic intervention and the giants were destroyed by extraterrestrials from space.

The legend gives a mind-gripping account of giants who arrived on South American shores in huge balsa boats made of rushes. The astonished natives hiding nearby only came up to their kneecaps. These 'Goliaths' had formidable appearances reminding one of monsters: they were beardless, shaggy haired, and eyes the size of saucers shone from their massive heads. Some were dressed in animal skins, others were naked. And they were without women.

On landing they made a primitive settlement and with incredible herculean strength dug wells through solid rock for water. The wells, lined with masonry, stood for centuries. However, these enormous creatures upset the surrounding ecology by eating so much and exhausting resources. Their appetites were said to be fifty times that of one of the natives and enormous quantities of sea fish were destroyed to satisfy their ravishing hunger. Uncivilized and ruthless, they were feared and hated by the natives; but the natives were not strong enough to resist these horrible creatures who had conquered their land, resulting in the giants occupying the territory for a good many years.

Since they lacked women, they turned inward and became homosexual, practising sodomy with each other openly. The natives declared that because of this they were punished by God. The legend has extraterrestrial overtones with its conclusion stating that when the giants were all together and indulging in their perversions devastating fire came down from the heavens accompanied by deafening noise. Suddenly from the chaos a shining angel appeared and slew them in a single blow, followed by an inferno of fire that quickly consumed them.

The angel in this legend may be a celestial in a spaceship that emits some sort of flaming weaponry. The legend may be giving us a clue to the last days of the Taurus giants in South America.

# TWELVE

# Taurus Structures in the World

IT IS POSSIBLE the world has many megalithic structures left by the Taurus giants and a good example are the trenches known as the Foggaras of Adrar. They consist of a network of wide passages dug sometimes as much as 250 feet below the surface of the desert, and passing through miles of country to collect water from reservoirs in the subsoil formed by the very rare rains that fall in the Sahara on an average of once in ten years.

The tunnels are ventilated at intervals by shafts called seggias. The desert people are trained to look after them but no person knows who their original builders were. The foggaras are a megalithic work and architecturally as mysterious as the great pyramids of antiquity. They also remind us of Atlantis and the megalithic trenches built by Poseidon, the Taurus giant.

Another structure the herculean Taurus giants may have left is the cyclopean terrace of Baalbek in the mountains of Lebanon which has huge blocks of stone weighing more than a thousand tons. No one has ever been able to give a convincing explanation for the terrace of Baalbek. However, Russian Professor Agrest considers it possible that the terrace is the remains of a gigantic airfield. If he is right, perhaps this is the very place that major landings from and take-offs to the Pleiades actually took place. Forty thousand workers would be needed to move this huge mass. One wonders how such a multitude could have access to the slab in order to lift it. Moreover, this supreme superstructure cannot be raised by any known means in today's world.

Another structure worthy of mention is India's Black Pagoda.

F

On top of a 228-foot-high temple rests a single stone slab 25 feet thick, with an estimated weight of 2,000 tons. The mind is expanded to the utmost trying to imagine the complicated pulley system or platforms for thousands of slaves to move a four million pound monolith to a perch 228 feet above the ground. It seems more plausible that this structure was made possible through the technological skills and superior strength of the Taurus giants rather than the obvious limitations of earthmen. We are reminded of Plato's description of Poseidon, the giant from Taurus, when he sets out alone to create massive projects on Atlantis: ". . . and Poseidon himself set in order with ease, as a god would, the central island. . . ."

Supreme amongst the mysteries of antiquity, unrivalled by the achievements of later architects and builders, the great Pyramid of Gizeh may bear mute witness to the Taurus civilization on Earth, which, having completed its predestined span, passed into oblivion or returned to space. The greatest architectural achievement of the Taurus giants may be the great Pyramid of Gizeh. A clue to the purpose of the great Pyramid may lie in Plato's opening lines of his Atlantis account when he mentions that the gods divided our world amongst themselves. In order to divide the world amongst themselves they may have taken an aerial survey and pinpointed the centre of the world's land mass. In this case it happened to be the Egyptian desert. On this location they built a huge planet marker, or cosmic survey post. It accurately sat in the centre of the world through intricate calculations of the heavens and Earth. Today it is still visible and known as the great Pyramid at Gizeh. The other pyramids that followed may have been only smaller imitations of Gizeh and served other functions.

The site of this inter-galactic focal point may be more important than its amazing construction. It stands exactly in the centre of the world land map, its edges diverge from the four cardinal points by only a few minutes. This precision must have been obtained by a survey of our Earth from space. To fix this focal position the celestials must have surveyed our Earth from space, made a global map projected flat and penetrated the centre of our land surface at the Nile delta.

The superior design of the Great Pyramid falls in line with our theory of the Taurus giants and their megalithic structures on Earth. It is an artificial mountain some 490 feet high, and weighs 6,500,000 tons. Surely this was not built as a burial place for a lone earthman who proclaimed himself king, as scholars have stated throughout the ages. Its structure and location leave us to believe that there is something much more profound at stake than that. Perhaps the Great Pyramid was first designed in the Pleiades—400 light years from Earth. And the Taurus astronauts took their plans by spaceship to our world and erected the highly precise superstructure as a planet marker.

Earthly explanations do not give satisfactory answers as to: "who were the illumined mathematicians who planned its parts and dimensions, the master craftsmen who supervised its construction or the skilled artisans who trued its blocks of stone."

Manly P. Hall in *The Secret Teachings of All Ages* sheds some interesting light on the Great Pyramid. In referring to Herodotus he states:

While his account is extremely colourful, it is apparent that the Father of History, for reasons which he doubtless considered sufficient, concocted a fraudulent story to conceal the true origin and purpose of the Great Pyramid. This is but one of several instances in his writings which would lead the thoughtful reader to suspect that Herodotus himself was an initiate of the Sacred Schools and consequently obligated to preserve inviolate the secrets of the ancient orders. The theory advanced by Herodotus and now generally accepted that the Pyramid was the tomb of the Pharaoh Cheops cannot be substantiated. In fact, Manetho, Eratosthenes, and Diodorus Siculus all differ from Herodotus—as well as from each other—regarding the name of the builder of this supreme edifice. The sepulchral vault, which, according to the Lepsius Law of pyramid construction, should have been finished at the same time as the monument or sooner, was never completed. There is no proof that the building was erected by the Egyptians, for the elaborate carvings with which the burial chambers of Egyptian royalty are almost invariably ornamented are entirely lacking and it embodies none of the elements of their architecture or decoration, such as inscriptions, images, cartouches, paintings, and other distinctive features associated with dynastic mortuary art.

As well as megalithic structures the world is filled with legends and archaeological finds of the giants themselves. Many traditions agree that the Atlanteans were giants. Others have wondered if they came from some other planet and perhaps were the men who built the cyclopean cities and sculpted the rock figures mentioned in Daniel Ruzo's description of the Masma civilization. In the Hava Supai Canyon was found a rock carving of a giant human fighting a mammoth. In California and Arizona skeletons of giants twelve feet tall having six toes have been unearthed, suggesting visitors from another planet or an ancient race of men such as Taurus humanoids. In his excavations in Moravia, the archaeologist Burkhaltar found stone tools more than ten feet long, weighing three to four hundred pounds. Evidence showed they were tools that had been used!

The Okenagan Indians of British Columbia tell an interesting legend which evokes the destruction of Atlantis. Long ago in mid ocean existed Sama-tumi-whooah, meaning 'White Man's Island', whose white giants were ruled by a tall queen called Scomalt. After ages of peace the giants warred, killing each other. The angry queen severed that portion of the island inhabited by the wicked giants and floated it to sea. The floating island broke up and all the people drowned except one man and one woman. But before the island sank they built a raft and sailed away to America, and came to Okenagan country. This legend may be a distorted reflection of the Taurus giants on Atlantis.

Through the ages, stone circles like Stonehenge were built all over the world perhaps with interplanetary significance to our solar system and its sister solar system in the Pleiades. F. W. Holiday suggests that megalithic structures in the U.K. are astronomically linked to the Pleiades. Stanzas in Asiatic literature mention a towering giant, the astronomer and magician Asurmaya, said to be an Atlantean who had a great advanced knowledge of the stars.

Stonehenge, situated on Salisbury Plain, is pre-eminent amongst megalithic structures in the British Isles. How these huge masses of rock were erected has not been satisfactorily explained. Might these big stones be another of the Taurus structures on Earth?

The Druids who have been associated with the stones, having practised ceremonies amongst them, had as their symbol the Taurus Cross fashioned out of an oak tree. Often the sacrifice of a white bull was made under the tree – a ritual that sounds like a direct connection to the Taurus constellation. It is alleged that the Druids can be traced back to Baccshic and Eleusinian mysteries in Greece or the Egyptian rites of Isis and Osiris that probably had Atlantis or Pleiades origins. Sun worship, associated by some scholars with the Atlantis empire, played a part in their rituals.

The Pleiades influence in our architecture may have continued long after the Taurus giants disappeared. If masonry can be traced back to Atlantis, and Atlantis to the Pleiades as we mention later in Chapter 15, 'The Pleiades and our Institutions', Masonic structures may have been cosmically inspired. Manly P. Hall declares:

Masonic symbols are to be found on the stones of numerous public buildings not only in England and on the continent but also in Asia. In his *Indian Masons' Marks of the Mogul Dynasty*, A. Goraham describes scores of markings appearing on the walls of buildings such as the Tajmahal, the Jama Masjid and that famous Masonic structure, the Kutab Minar. According to those who regard Masonry as an outgrowth of the secret society of architects and builders which for thousands of years formed a cast of master craftsmen, Chiram Abiff was the Tyrian Grand Master of a world wide organisation of artisans, with headquarters in Tyre. Then philosophy consisted in incorporating in the measurements and ornamentation of temples, palaces, mausoleums, fortresses, and other public buildings their knowledge of the laws controlling the universe. Every initiated workman was given a hieroglyphic with which he marked the stones. He tried to show to all posterity

85

that he thus dedicated to the Supreme Architect of the Universe each perfected product of his labour.

Concerning Masonic marks, Robert Freke Gould writes :

It is very remarkable that these marks are to be found in all countries—in the chambers of the Great Pyramid at Gizeh, on the underground walls of Jerusalem, in Herculaneum and Pompeii, on Roman walls and Grecian temples, in Hindustan, Mexico, Peru, Asia Minor as well as the great ruins of England, France, Germany, Scotland, Italy, Portugal and Spain.

# THIRTEEN

# *Taurus and the* Odyssey

THE OLDEST STORY that we know is called 'The Ship-wrecked Sailor', and was written in Egypt 2,500 years before the birth of Jesus. The idea of Sinbad the Sailor may have been taken from it. But the oldest real books are the *Iliad* and the *Odyssey*, supposed to have been composed by the Greek poet Homer between 800 and 1,000 years before the Christian era. Perhaps he brought together the work of other poets as well as his own. Homer's actual existence was debated in the nineteenth century but most recent scholars say such a poet actually lived. Legend says that he was blind and that seven cities (the Pleiades number again) claimed him. His narrative poems, the *Iliad* and the *Odyssey*, are masterpieces and models for all later epics.

The most important thing is not so much the existence of Homer but the origins of the source material from which these poems were put together. There might be a great deal of fact mixed with fiction, and here lies our challenge to separate them in order to find the historical truth.

Even if we concede that the *Odyssey* is pure fantasy it is probably very close to something very powerful. When Walt Disney drew a talking duck with a sailor suit it was pure fantasy. Nonetheless it was based on millions of real live ducks that exist on the Earth. In the same way as the 'Disney analogy', the real live gods (extraterrestrials) may be looming very close to Homer's classic if they are not at times accurately recorded in it.

If the *Odyssey* is not pure fantasy there are only two possibilities. It is a true story or it is partly true and partly fiction. If it is a true story the reason we may have trouble understanding it is through the distortion of time. Time knows only an infinite array of expressions and forms throughout the universe, and through this process facts dissolve into mythology to those who are too far removed from them. Today's facts are the unbelievable essence of a distant future.

Perhaps this is what is happening in the *Odyssey*. The real setting for the story could have been at the time of Plato's Atlantis (9560 B.C.), and the *Odyssey* was allegedly written much later in 900 B.C. Through the *Odyssey* we may be watching how mythology is born. We see the gods as people but slowly dissolving into the elements of nature. This makes it different from the Atlantis account which I believe is a document from which a great deal of the world's mythology has sprung. However, Plato said that if Homer was not a poet he would have been a great historian and here could lie an important clue that the *Odyssey* may also contain more truth than we realize.

The extraterrestrial, Poseidon, is mentioned a great deal throughout the *Odyssey*, receiving symbols of sacrifice representing the Taurus constellation. He is first introduced in the story as being connected with Ethiopia, and this may be a hint that Poseidon was in Africa: "Howbeit Poseidon had now departed for distant Ethiopians, the Ethiopians that are sundered in twain, the uttermost of men, abiding some where Hyperion sinks and some where he rises. There he looked to receive his hecatomb of bulls and rams. . . ."

In the first paragraph of Book 3 we view a similar scene:

Now the sun arose and left the lovely mere, speeding to the brazen heaven, to give light to the immortals and to mortal men on the earth, the grain-giver, and they reached Pylos, the established castle of Neleus. There the people were doing sacrifice on the seashore, slaying black bulls without spor to the dark-haired god, the shaker of the earth. Nine companies there were, and five hundred men sat in each, and in every company they held nine bulls ready to hand. Just as they had tasted the inner parts, and were burning slices of the thighs on the altar to the god.

In Book 13 the Phaecians may be enacting their linkage to the Taurus constellation through Poseidon :

And the Phaecians state : "Cease ye from the convoy of mortals, whosoever any shall come unto our town, and let us sacrifice to Poseidon twelve choice bulls, if perchance he may take pity, neither overshadow our city with a great mountain.

And further on we see more evidence of what might be a Taurus ceremony being carried out :

And a shrill wind arose and blew, and the ships ran most fleetly over the teeming ways, and in the night they touched at Geraestus. So there we sacrifice many thighs of bulls to Poseidon, for joy that we had measured out so great a stretch of sea.

Poseidon is referred to as deathless. This could mean that extraterrestrials on Earth had a longer life span than earth people : "We may pour forth before Poseidon and the other deathless gods"; and later their broad relationship to the universe is mentioned : "the deathless gods, who keep the wide heaven."

There is further evidence in the *Odyssey* of giants which correlates with the Bible, the Book of Enoch and the Atlantis account :

First Nausithous was son of Poseidon, the Earth-shaker, and of Periboea, the comeliest of women, youngest daughter of the great-hearted Eurymedon, who once was king among the haughty Giants. Howbeit, he destroyed his infatuate people, and was himself destroyed; but Poseidon lay with Periboea and begat a son, proud Nausithous, who sometime was prince among the Phaeacians.

This description of Poseidon could be a distortion from the Atlantis story when he married Cleito, or Poseidon had other sexual relationships on earth. However it contains a more important clue. The passage suggests he was connected to Phaecia which may have been Atlantis.

The *Odyssey* may be offering a clue how Poseidon went into mythology as a sea god. The Atlantis account states shipping was not in existence in our world until the arrival of Poseidon. Poseidon taught earth people the art of sailing and this could be revealed to us in Book 7 when Athene says to Odysseus while visiting Phaecia: "They pin their faith on the clippers that carry them across the far-flung seas, for Poseidon has made them a sailor folk, and these ships of theirs are as swift as a bird or as thought itself." This may be how thousands of years later this real celestial dissolved into mythology as the god of the sea.

That the extraterrestrials themselves are giants might be revealed to us in Book 7:

> For always heretofore the gods appear manifest amongst us, when-so ever we offer glorious hecatombs, and they feast by our side, sitting at the same board, yea, and even if a wayfarer going all alone has met with them, they use no disguise, since we are near of kin to them, even as the Cyclopes and the wild tribes of Giants.

There are references in the *Odyssey* that the Taurus giant, Poseidon, is of dark complexion, such as this passage in Book 9: "So I spake and then he prayed to the Lord Poseidon stretching forth his hands to the starry heaven: 'hear me Poseidon, girdler of the earth, god of the dark hair'."

During the story Odysseus encounters a giant who devours his men; at first glance this seems like a fairytale but the Book of Enoch soberly states that before their destruction the giants eventually became degenerate and ate human flesh.

There are interesting passages throughout the *Odyssey* concerning the Phaecians who appear to be descendants of extraterrestrials: "Nay, he shall sail on a well-bound raft, in sore distress, and on the twentieth day arrive at fertile Scheria, even at the land of the Phaeacians, who are near kin to the gods." (Book 5)

And in Book 6 we are given a description of their country: "Meanwhile Athene went to the land and the city of Phaeacians, who of old, upon a time, dwelt in spacious Hypereia; near the Cyclopes they dwelt, men exceeding proud, who harried them continually, being mightier than they."

The setting of Phaecia further comes to life:

But when we set foot within the city,—whereby goes a high wall with towers, and there is a fair haven on either side of the town, and narrow is the entrance, and curved ships are drawn up on either hand of the mole, for all the folk have stations for their vessels, each man one for himself. And there is the place of assembly about the goodly temple of Poseidon, furnished with heavy stones, deep bedded in the earth.

Passages such as this add credence to Plato's Atlantis recital because we can clearly see that Plato did not invent the name Poseidon and that Poseidon was worshipped by many before Plato's birth.

In Book 13 there is a passage where Poseidon is speaking, claiming his linkage to the Phaecians: "Father Zeus, I for one shall no longer be worshipped among the deathless gods, when mortal men hold me in no regard, even Phaeacians, who moreover are of mine own lineage."

Perhaps Phaecia was part of Atlantis and consistent with our theory that the region was at Tarshish. We note here Poseidon's reverence for Zeus. The *Odyssey* is consistent with Atlantis in its many references to Zeus as a god (extraterrestrial) superior to the other gods. There are also passages throughout that are consistent with our Atlantis theory that royalty was caused from extraterrestrials mixing with people of the Earth. Such an example is in Book 4:

Taste ye food and be glad, and thereafter when ye have supped we will ask what men ye are; for the blood of your parents is not lost in you, but ye are of the line of men that are sceptred kings, the fosterlings of Zeus; for no churls could beget sons like you.

A later chapter will present a theory that Zeus dwelt on a planet in the Pleiades and established his Taurus empire on Earth through celestials like Poseidon. This passage is in line with our theory of celestial intervention causing royalty as it pertains to the Atlantis account.

The Pleiades are only mentioned by name once throughout the story when Odysseus sets his sails by them:

And goodly Odysseus rejoices as he sets his sails to the breeze. So he sat and cunningly guided the craft with the helm, nor did sleep fall upon his eyelids as he viewed the Pleiads and Boötes, that setteth late, and the Bear, which they likewise call the Wain, which turneth even in one place, and keepeth watch upon Orion, and alone hath no part in the baths of Ocean.

However, we might be getting our clues to the constellation of Taurus through other indirect means: the presence of Poseidon, the sacrifice of bulls, the giants and powerful allegory such as the following sentences contained in Book 19 :

Twain are the gates of shadowy dreams, the one is fashioned of horn and one of ivory. Such dreams as pass through the portals of sawn ivory are deceitful, and bear tidings that are unfulfilled. But the dreams that come forth through the gates of polished horn bring a true issue, whosoever of mortals beholds them.

The ivory could refer to a substance being relative to Earth and those who choose their learning solely from the world are limited. The gates of the "polished horn" might represent the bull of the Taurus constellation and those that seek this passage receive cosmic wisdom.

## FOURTEEN

# The Pleiades and the Bible

MANLY P. HALL states:

The Apocalypse or Book of Revelation now incorporated in the New Testament, popularly accredited to St. John the Divine—is by far the most important but least understood of the Gnostic christian writings. Though Justin Martyr declared the Book of Revelation to have been written by John one of Christ's apostles, its authorship was disputed as early as the second century after Christ. In the third century these contentions became acute.

The Pleiades could be mentioned a great deal by allegory in this work of unknown authorship and it may be worth speculation that its origins were influenced by celestials from Taurus. The generally accepted theory that the Book of Revelation was the actual record of a mystical experience of John when he was in exile in the Isle of Patmos (the Johannine theory) is now regarded with more disfavour amongst critical scholars. New theories relative to the space age may be worthy of consideration at this time—an approach in harmony with Jerome who centuries ago declared : "The intrinsic value of the book lies in its 'universal mystery'."

Like Atlantis, unless another dimension is added to the Apocalyse, theologians and scholars will have trouble coping with this work, for by earthbound theories this mystic writing appears to be only a phantasmagoria of divine inspiration.

The Pleiades are only mentioned directly twice in the Bible when Job giving reverence to God states in Job 9 : 9 : "which maketh Arcturus, Orion and Pleiades, and the chambers of the

93

south"; and in Job 38 : 31 when the Lord is speaking to Job : "Have you fitted a curb to the Pleiades?" (American translation). In verse 33 God says : "Do you know the ordinances of the heavens; can you put into effect their plans on earth?"

The Book of Revelation does not mention the Pleiades by name but mentions the seven stars : like the Book of Enoch the number seven runs in succession throughout which could be further allegorical reference to the Pleiades. Manly P. Hall states :

> The sixth to eleventh chapters are devoted to an account of the opening of the seven seals on the book held by the lamb. When the seventh seal was broken there was a space for about half an hour. Then came forth seven angels and to each was given a trumpet. When the seven angels sounded their trumpets intoned the seven lettered name of logos—great catastrophes ensued. A star which was called wormwood, fell from heaven, thereby signifying that the secret doctrine of the ancients had been given to men who had profaned it and had caused the wisdom of God to become a destructive agency."

Manly P. Hall further states : "The fifteenth to sixteenth chapters inclusive contain an account of the seven angels (the Pleiades) who pour their vials upon the earth. The contents of their vials (the loosened energy of the cosmic bull) are called the seven last plagues."

The Book of Revelation is probably not a book of the future but a prehistoric text, existing long before our time, referring to Atlantis and the first wave of civilization. Cosmic initiators such as Poseidon brought forth a new wave of civilization in this planet based on the precepts of cosmic wisdom. It flourished on a high moral plane exactly as the Atlantis account states and then went into decay. Its decadence may have caused those who created it to destroy it, and a good part of the prehistoric world may have been destroyed by Pleiades celestials.

As well as strong references to the seven stars, the Bible mentions giants, which correlates with our theory of giants being from the Pleiades. We find in Genesis 6 the statement that "there were giants in the earth in those days". In Deuteronomy 3 : 11 we read that : "Only Og, King of Bashan remained of the remnants of giants" and that his bedstead measured nine cubits by four (a cubit being about 18 inches) and in I Samuel 17 is reference to Goliath, whose height was "six cubits and a span". Reference is also made in Numbers 13, Joshua 12, 13, 15 and 17, and II Samuel 21. These passages do not present a fantasia of characters but are written in an historical style, and are not introduced on any mythological terms. They come from religious scholars of diverse time periods and seem to be stated as facts, and if they were to be extracted they would in no way interrupt the text, even though they are widely scattered throughout.

These passages in the Bible are in harmony with the ancient folklore of many of the world's nations. The Jotunheim of Norway have sagas of towering giants that dwelt in the slopes of the Scandinavian mountains. Giants are recorded in the mythical traditions of ancient Mediterranean races, Tibetans, Hindus, Australians, Chaldeans, Hebrews, and North and South American Indians.

Genesis is very much in accord with my theory of the Taurus giant Poseidon in Atlantis and the giants in the Book of Enoch. Poseidon's wife Cleito, the earth woman, may be represented in Chapter 6 : 1 before the arrival of Poseidon : "And it came to pass, when men began to multiply on the face of the earth, and daughters were born unto them. . . ." Further we read : "That the sons of God saw the daughters of men they were fair; and they took them wives of all which they chose." Also : "There were giants in the earth in those days; and also after that, when the sons of God came unto the daughters of men, and they bare children to them, the same became mighty men which were of old, men of renown."

These passages could be chronologically correct for my Atlantis theory. First, the giants such as Poseidon are here from space. After that his offspring Atlas, Gaderius, etc., the sons of God (Poseidon) or 'gods' from the Jewish plural 'Elohim', married earth women and a high degree of civilization came forward exactly as stated in Atlantis.

95

Verse 5 may refer to the decay of the giants' civilization in accordance with the Book of Enoch: "And God saw the wickedness of man was great in the earth, and that every imagination of the thoughts of his heart was only evil continually." This may have led to cosmic intervention to purify the world by a flood. Certain initiates such as Noah may have been saved in order for the world to start a new civilization.

It seems strange that the tradition of the flood would last for such a great length of time amongst so many diverse nations in the world, if it is not for the fact that it is based on an actual event. There have been many floods on this planet and most of the stories connected with them are soon vanished, but the central theme of the biblical flood has survived, leading us to suspect its authenticity.

If the Atlantis account, the Book of Enoch, and the Bible are all basically correct and in harmony with one another, then we may have an unbroken chain of recorded history since 9560 B.C. If they coincide, all three books may go back that far if the Egyptian priests were right about the date of the Atlantis story. Unfortunately we have little concrete evidence that far back to substantiate this and Atlantis itself has not been found.

The experience Moses had on Mount Sinai may yet be another case of intervention by Pleiades celestials on earth as stated in Exodus 19:16: "And it came to pass on the third day in the morning, that there were thunders and lightnings, and a thick cloud upon the mount, and the voices of the trumpet exceeding loud, so that all the people that was in the camp trembled." And in Exodus 19:20: "And the Lord came down upon Mount Sinai, on top of the Mount; and Moses went up."

The following could be a description of a spaceship coming down on Mount Sinai. Possibly because of radiation emanating from the craft, the captain warns the people to stand back. However it is not clear how Moses is protected: "And the Lord said unto Moses, Go down, charge the people lest they break through unto the Lord to gaze, and many of them perish." [Exodus 20:21]

96

Then the Lord gave Moses the Ten Commandments, followed by various divers laws and ordinances :

Exodus 24 : 12—"And the Lord said unto Moses come up to me into the mount, and be there : and I will give thee tables of stone, and a law, and commandments which I have written; that thou mayest teach them."

13—"And Moses rose up, and his minister Joshua : and Moses went up into the mount of God."

14—"And he said unto the elders, Tarry ye here for us, until we come again unto you : and behold, Aaron and Hur are with you : if any man have any matters to do, let him come unto them."

15—"And Moses went up into the mount, and a cloud covered the mount."

16—"And the Glory of the Lord abode upon Mount Sinai, and the the cloud covered it six days : and the seventh day he called unto Moses out of the midst of a cloud."

17—"And the sight of the glory of the Lord was like devouring fire on the top of the mount in the eyes of the children of Israel."

18—"And Moses went into the midst of the cloud, and gat him up into the mount : and Moses was in the mount forty days and forty nights."

There may be an important clue in Exodus 27 : 1–2 and 29 : 12 that the Ten Commandments came from the constellation of Taurus. The Lord instructs Moses to build an altar containing horns, a symbol of the Taurus constellation. The last sentences remind us of the 'bull' ceremony that took place on Atlantis :

1 – "And thou shalt make an altar of Shit-tim wood, five cubits long and five cubits broad; the altar shall be four square : and the height thereof shall be three cubits."

2—"And thou shalt make the horns of it upon the four corners thereof : his horns shall be of the same : and thou shalt overlay it with brass."

12—"And thou shalt take of the blood of the bullock, and put it upon the horns of the altar with thy finger, and pour all the blood beside the bottom of the altar."

Manly P. Hall states :

According to certain Jewish mystics, Moses ascended Mount Sinai three times, remaining in the presence of God forty days each time. During the first forty days the tables of the written law were delivered to the prophet; during the second forty days he received the soul of the law; and during the last forty days God instructed him in the laws of the Qabbalah, the soul of the soul of the law. Moses concealed in the first four books of the Pentateuch the secret instructions that God had given him, and for centuries students of Qabbalism have sought therein the secret doctrine of Israel. As the spiritual nature of man is concealed in the physical body so the unwritten law—the Mishna and Qabbalah is concealed within the written teachings of the Mosaic code. Qabbalah means the secret of hidden tradition, the unwritten law, and according to an early rabbi, it was delivered to man in order that through the aid of its abstruse principles he might learn to understand the mystery of both the universe about him and the universe within him.

The origin of Qabbalism is a legitimate subject for controversy. Early initiates of the Qabbalistic mysteries believed that its principles were first taught by God to a school of his angels before the fall of man. The angels later communicated the secrets of Adam, so that through the knowledge gained from an understanding of its principles fallen humanity might gain its lost estate. The angel Raziel dispatched from heaven to instruct Adam in the mysteries of the Qabbalah. Different angels were employed to initiate the succeeding patriarchs in this difficult science. Tophiel was the teacher of Shem, Raphael of Isaac, Metatron of Moses and Michael of David etc.

Manly P. Hall states further :

While upon the heights of Mount Sinai, Moses received from Jehovah two tablets bearing the characters of the Decalogue traced by the very finger of Israel's god. These tablets were fashioned from the divine sapphire, which the Most High after removing from his throne, had cast into the abyss to become the foundation and generator of the worlds. The sacred stone formed by heavenly dew was sundered by the breath of God, and upon the two parts were drawn in black fire the figures of the law. These precious inscriptions aglow with celestial splendour were delivered by the Lord on the Sabbath Day into the hands of Moses, who was able to read the illumined letters from the reverse side because of the transparency of the great jewel.

Manly P. Hall claims that when Moses received the stone tablets they were representative of the universe, the higher or celestial sphere. He deemed the people unworthy of receiving them and had them destroyed, replacing them with stone tablets containing more basic commandments. Thus universal truth returned to heaven, leaving only its shadow with the twelve tribes.

Manly P. Hall claims these laws from heaven were symbolized in King Solomon's temple :

The right tablet of the law further signifies Jachin the white pillar of light; the left tablet Boaz—the shadowy pillar of darkness. These were the names of the two pillars cast from brass set up on the porch of King Solomon's temple. They were eighteen cubits in height and beautifully ornamented with wreaths of chainwork, nets and pomegranates. On the top of each pillar was a large bowl—now erroneously called a ball or globe—one of the bowls probably containing fire and the other water. The celestial globe (originally the bowl of fire) surmounting the right hand column (Jachin) symbolised the divine man : the terrestrial globe (the bowl of water) surmounting the left hand column (Boaz) signified the earthly man.

# FIFTEEN

# The Pleiades and our Institutions

OUR FIRST TRADITIONS concerning the Pleiades may go back to Atlantis when many of our institutions were founded by the Taurus giant, Poseidon. The Atlantis account states it was through him that the world knew its first concepts of shipping, commerce and institutions. However to what extent these original concepts survived after the flood is not certain.

Many of our concepts of religion and royalty may be due to the influence of the Pleiades through Atlantis. The descendants of Poseidon built a temple sacred to him and his earth wife. At this point Poseidon and Cleito are deceased and will be carried through the traditions of religion. This may be our first record of religion in the world as we know it. The story runs close to the Christian tradition of an earth virgin being impregnated by an extraterrestrial and the offspring being a superior being. We note in this case that the offspring became royalty which may be how royalty began in our world. As stated elsewhere in this book royalty was formed by the descendants of Poseidon and Cleito being half extraterrestrials and half earth children:

> In the centre there stood a temple sacred to Cleito and Poseidon, which was reserved as holy ground, and encircled with a wall of gold; this being the very spot where at the beginning they had generated and brought to birth the family of ten royal lines. [Plato]

Atlas, being the first born, formed the first royal branch on our planet ("conceding the leadership to the royal branch of Atlas"). Many of our fraternities and law institutions may have also started here when the princes put on their sable robes and received judgement from each other. If extraterrestrial intervention, royalty, religion, government and laws all go back to Atlantis, then it is maybe the root of all Western civilization. And the social structure of Atlantis, through its initiator Poseidon, the Taurus giant, may go back 400 light years from Earth to the Pleiades.

This intervention of Poseidon into our world may be in harmony with universal law. Professor Andre Bougenac notes that in most plant species, in which evolution is more rapid, fecundation requires the coming of a 'foreigner', an external agent, such as the wind, insects or man, which transports pollen usually by air. This analogy may apply to Poseidon, a foreign agent, who came to fecundate Earth, an earthly woman and our intelligences. An event such as the 'Poseidon Adventure' may be symbolic of hybridization, transplants and mixtures necessary to the evolution of species throughout the domains of the cosmos. The universe may cross-index her species.

If the Atlantis dates are correct the constellation of Taurus may have been established on Earth in 9560 B.C. "The Taurus sign has been associated with the animal Adam first offered in sacrifice. Official records show the observation of the constellation also going back into antiquity. *Le Taureau* of France, *Il Toro* of Italy, and *Der Stier* of Germany, everywhere Taurus was one of the earliest and most noted constellations. We find it making the Vernal Equinox from about 4000 to 1700 B.C. in the golden age of archaic astronomy; in all the ancient zodiacs preserved to us it began the year." (Richard S. Allen)

The Cabiric mysteries of Samothrace were renowned amongst the ancients, being next to the Elysian in public esteem. Herodotus states that the Samothracians received their doctrines from the Pelasgians. Little is known concerning the Cabiric rituals. Some refer to the Cabiri (heaven above) as seven in number and refer to them as the seven spirits of fire before the throne of Saturn. Others believe the Cabiri to be seven sacred wonders called planets. Seven heavenly spheres are mentioned a great deal in ancient literature as spirits, etc., and have been taken to be the seven planets, but I think in many cases it means the Pleiades. Professor Homet made a similar observation concerning the disc of Phaistos.

In the Eleusinian mysteries and the rites of Mithras the candidate ascended the seven rungs of a ladder or climbed the seven steps of a pyramid. They also had rituals to master spheres and to reunite them with the divine source of his own nature.

Herodotus reveals to us that the ancient city of Ecbatana had seven walls and coloured to the seven planets. If we could go back in time and observe this more carefully we might find these seven walls commemorated the Pleiades. The Ziggurat or astronomical tower of the god Nebo at Borsippa ascended in seven great steps or stages. In India, one of the Mogul emperors constructed a fountain with seven levels. In the mysteries of the seven logi, or creative lords, are shown as streams of force issuing from the mouth of Eteindone. This signifies the spectrum being extracted from the white light of the supreme deity. The seven creators or fabricators of the inferior spheres were called by the Jews the Elohim (gods).

Manly P. Hall states: "The seven planetary circulations are represented in the circumambulations of the Masonic Lodge; by the marching of the Jewish priests seven times around the walls of Jericho, and the Mohammedan priests seven times around the Kabba and Mecca." This may be based on the fact that only seven planets were known at that time, or it may be symbolic worship to the seven Pleiades.

"An early Grecian gem shows three nude figures, hand in hand, standing on the head of the bull, one pointing to seven stars in line over the back, which Landseer referred to as the Hyades; but as six of the stars are strongly cut, and one but faintly so, and the letter P is superscribed, Dr Charles Anthon is undoubtedly correct in claiming them to be the Pleiades." (Richard S. Allen)

A mithraic sculpture shows Mithras leaning on the recumbent form of a bull into whose throat he is drawing a sword. The interpretation by Manly P. Hall is "that the bull is esoterically the constellation of Taurus . . . Mithras, entering into the side of the bull, slays the celestial creature and nourishes the universe with its blood."

A coin minted in 43 B.C. depicted Clodius Turnius and the Pleiades as a symbol. Earlier still (312–64 B.C.), the Seleucidae of Syria placed the humped bull in a position of attack on their coins as a symbol of this constellation. Taurus is shown on the gold muhrs and zodiacal rupees of Jehanger Shah of India in 1618. A very ancient coin of Samos, perhaps of the sixth century before Christ, bears a half kneeling sectional figure of a bull with a lion's head on the obverse; and another coin of Thuri, in Lucania, of the fourth century B.C., has the complete animal in a position of charge. Another coin of this same city bears the bull with a bird on its back. (Richard S. Allen)

After Egyptian worship of the bull-god Osiris had spread to other Mediterranean countries, Taurus became his sky representative, as also of his mother Isis. Perhaps Isis was one of the space travellers who came to earth with Poseidon, and like Atlantis her descendants worshipped her in Egypt through the cult of the bull.

Isis is often shown with her son Osiris in her arms. She is crowned with a lunar orb, ornamented with the horns of a bull —a clue that she may have been a Pleiades celestial. Another associate from Taurus on this planet may have been Thoth Hermes Trismegistus, the founder of Egyptian learning:

This wise man of the ancient world is said to have given the priests and philosophers the secrets that have been presented to this day in myth and legend. Scholars believe that he imparted cosmic truths to initiates of mystery schools but were concealed from the illiterate. The mystery of Hermeticism, and the wisdom of Egypt are believed by some to be epitomised in the sphinx, which has preserved its secrets from the secrets of a hundred generations. (Manley P. Hall)

"The Taurus constellation is said to have begun the zodiacal series on walls of a sepulchral chamber in the Ramesseum; and its stars certainly were made much of throughout all Egyptian history and religion, not only from its then containing the vernal equinox, but from the belief that the human race was created when the sun was here"—a legend possibly stemming from when the Taurus initiators recreated the civilization of the human race on earth.

Richard S. Allen further says :

Representations of the Mithraic bull on gems of four or five centuries before Christ prove that Taurus was at that time still prominent in Persico-Babylonian astronomy as well as in its religions. One of these representations shows the front of the Bull's head—the symbol of the universe. Earlier in Akkadia Taurus seems to have been known as the Bull of Light, its double title, Te Te, referring to its two groups, the Hyades and Pleaides, which in every age have been of so much interest to mankind. A cylinder has the heavenly bull mentioned in connection with rain. The name of the second of the antediluvian Babylonian kings, the mythical Alaparos, seems connected with this constellation or with the lucida, Aldebaran; and its stars certainly were associated with the second month of the Assyrian year, A-aru, the Directing Bull, our April–May.

With the Druids Taurus was an important object of worship, their great religious festival, the Tauric being held when the sun entered its boundaries; and it has been claimed that perhaps the tors of England were the old sites of their taurine cult. A white bull was believed to have been used in the ceremonies of the Druids. It has been suggested by F. W. Holiday that Stonehenge and similar structures in England line up with the Pleiades. Stonehenge may have a very strong connection with the seven stars.

Astrologers made the Taurus sign the lord of man's neck, throat, and shoulders; Shakespeare having an amusing passage in *Twelfth Night*, in dialogue between Sir Toby Belch and Sir Andrew Aguecheek, when both blunder as to his character of Taurus. In all astrology Taurus has been thought eminently fortunate, portending riches and honour; and was one of the four royal stars, or guardians of the sky, of Persia 5,000 years ago, when it marked the vernal equinox. As such Flammarion quoted its title Taschter, which Lenormant said signified the Creator Spirit that caused rain and deluge.

The Narrow Cloudy Train of Female Stars of Manilius, and the Starry Seven, Old Atlas' Children, of Keats' *Endymion*, have everywhere been among the most noted objects in the history,

poetry and mythology of the heavens; though, as Aratos wrote of
the Pleiades:

> ... not a mighty space
> Holds all, and they themselves are dim to see.

In the fifth century before Christ Euripides mentioned the
Pleiades as nocturnal timekeepers; and Sappho, a century previously, marked the middle of the night by their setting. Centuries
still earlier Hesiod and Homer brought them into their most
beautiful verse; the former calling them Atlas-born, a reversal to
our theory that Atlas was 'Pleiades-born' through Poseidon on
earth. The Patriarch Job is thought to refer to them twice in his
word Kimah, a Cluster, or Heap, which the Hebrew herdsman-
prophet Amos also used. Again to quote Richard S. Allen:

The Hindus associated these stars with Agni, a god of fire. The
western Hindus held in the Pleiad month Kartik (October–
November) their great star festival 'Dibali', the feast of lamps.
This gave origin to the present feast of lanterns in Japan.

The title, written also Pliades and, in singular, Plias, has been
commonly derived from the Greek 'to sail', for it is believed the
heliacal rising of the group in May marked the opening of navigation to the Greeks, as its setting in late autumn did the close.
They shared a watery character always ascribed to the Hyades.
Ancient writers have used the word 'pliada' for showers, and rain
has been associated with their rising and setting.

A reference to the seasons is given in the *Work and Days:*

> When with their domes the slow-pac'd snails retreat,
> Beneath some foliage, from the burning heat
> Of the Pleiades, your tools prepare.

The bejewelled seven were a marked object on the Nile, and
supposed to represent the goddess Nit or Neith, the Shuttle, one of
the principal divinities of Lower Egypt, identified by the Greeks
with Athene, the Roman Minerva.

Perhaps like Poseidon and Osiris she was one of the group
who came from these stars.

"Grecian temples were oriented to them, or to their lucida; those
of Athene on the Acropolis, of different dates, to their correspond-

ingly different positions when rising. These were the temple of
1530 B.C.; the Hecatompedon of 1150 B.C.; and the great
Parthenon, finished on the same site 438 B.C. The temple of
Bacchus at Athens, 1030 B.C., looked towards their setting, as did
the Asclepieion at Epidaurus, 1275 B.C., and the temple at
Sunium of 845 B.C." One might wonder why so much Grecian
architecture was directed to such a small portion of the visible
sky if it were not for a connection between Athene and the seven
stars. "At some unknown date, perhaps contemporaneous with
these Grecian structures, they were pictured in the New World
on the walls of a Palenque temple upon a blue background; and
certainly were a well-known object in other parts of Mexico, for
Cortez heard there, in 1519, a very ancient tradition of the
destruction of the world in some past age at their midnight culmination." Perhaps more evidence that the Pleiades caused something much more dramatic on earth than the shedding of faint
rays of light. In order for the Pleiades to cause the destruction of
our world, beings from these stars would have to visit us.

Lewis Spence in *Myths of Mexico and Peru* states with what
fear the ancient Mexicans observed the voyage of these stars across
the zenith every fifty-two years:

With the conclusion of each period of fifty-two years a terrible
dread came upon the Mexicans that the world would come to an
end. A stated period of time had expired, a period that was regarded as fixed by divine command, and had been ordained that
on the completion of one of those series of fifty-two years earthly
time would cease and the universe be demolished. The Mexicans
then abandoned themselves to utmost prostration and the wicked
went about in terrible fear. As the first day of the fifty-third year
dawned the people narrowly observed the Pleiades, for if they
passed the zenith, time would proceed and the world would
become respited.

To return to Richard S. Allen:

Hesiod said that their appearance from the sun indicated the
approach of harvest, and their setting, autumn, the time for the
new sowing; while Aristotle wrote that honey was never gathered

before their rising. Nearly all classical poets and prose writers made like reference to them.

Mommsen found in their rising, from May–June, the occasion for the prehistoric festival, Athene's clothes-washing, at the beginning of the corn harvest, and the date for the annual election of the Achaeans; while Drach surmised that their midnight culmination in the time of Moses, ten days after the autumnal equinox, may have fixed the day of atonement on the 10th of Tishri.

Their rising in November marked the time for worship of deceased friends by the Parsis and Sabaeans, as also in the Druid's midnight rites of November. A recollection of it is found in the three holy days of our time, All Hallows Eve, All Saints Day and All Souls Day. Hippocrates made much of the Pleiades, dividing the year into four seasons based on their changing position in the heavens. And Caesar made their heliacal rising begin the Julian summer, and their cosmical setting the commencement of winter.

According to Manly P. Hall in *The Secret Teachings of All Ages*: "The sacred Pleiades were famous to freemasonry as the seven stars at the upper end of the sacred ladder."

If the Pleiades and Atlantis are associated there may be a connection between Masonry and the seven stars if the following by Manly P. Hall is correct: "Masonry came to Northern Africa from the lost continent of Atlantis, not under its present name, but under the general designation of sun and fire worship." And: "Freemasonry is more ancient than any of the world's religions." (One wonders if he is not getting a glimpse of the origins of Masonry on this planet in the Atlantis story when the princes enact a brotherhood amongst themselves after the cosmic bull ceremony.)

The universal significance of Masonry is noted by Mr Hall:

The best informed Masonic writers have realised that Solomon's Temple is a representation in miniature of the universal temple. Concerning this point, A. E. Waite, in a new encyclopaedia of Freemasonry writes: "It is macrocosmic in character, so that the temple is a symbol of the universe, a type of manifestation in itself."

The Sanctum Sanctorium of Freemasonry is ornamented with gnostic jewels of a thousand ages; its rituals ring with the divinely inspired words of seers and sages. A hundred religions have brought their gifts to its altar; arts and sciences unnumbered have contributed to its symbolism. Freemasonry is a world wide university, teaching the liberal arts and the sciences of the soul to all who will harken to its words. Its chairs are seals of learning and its pillars uphold an arch of universal education.

To return to Richard S. Allen :

In various ages the Pleiades have been taken for noteworthy groups of seven in philosophy or literature. This we see first in the Philosophical Pleiad of 620 to 550 B.C., otherwise known as the Seven Wise Men of Greece or the Seven Sages, generally given as Bias, Chilo, Cleobulus, Epimenides or Periander, Pittacus, Solon and the astronomer Thales; again in the Alexandrian Literary Pleiad, or the Tragic Pleiades, instituted in the third century B.C. by Ptolemy Philadelphus, and composed of the seven contemporary poets, variously given, but often as Apollonius of Rhodes, Callimachus or Philiscus, Homer the Younger of Hierapolis in Caria, Lycophron, Nicander, Theocritus, and Aratos; in the Literary Pleiad of Charlemagne, himself one of the Seven; in the Great Pleiade of France, of the sixteenth century brought together in the reign of Henri III and in the Lesser Pleiade, of inferior lights, in the subsequent reign of Louis XIII. Lastly appear the Pleiades of Connecticut, the seven patriotic poets after the Revolutionary War : Richard Alsop, Joel Barlow, Theodore Dwight, Timothy Dwight, Lemuel Hopkins, David Humphreys and John Trumball —all good men of Yale.

The Pleiades via Atlantis and the Mediterranean may have played a great part in the erection of human culture. It may be that all the perfection of civilization, and all the advancement made in philosophy, science and art amongst the ancients are due to those institutions, initiated by Taurus celestials, which under the veil of mystery sought to illustrate the sublimest truths of religion, morality and virtue, and impress them in the minds of their disciples. Before the celestial giants themselves went into decay on our planet and were destroyed in the Atlantean deluge they were probably of marvellous stature, "Men of Renown" according to the Bible. Their chief object may have been to teach the doctrine of one universal intelligence, the resurrection of man to eternal life, the dignity of the human soul, and to reveal to the people through astronomy and arcane secrets, the beauty, magnificence and splendour of the universe.

# SIXTEEN

# Our Record of a Speech
# Given in the Pleiades

OUR GALAXY the Milky Way of which we and the Pleiades are a part is 100,000 light years in diameter. Incredibly, there are more galaxies than there are grains of sand on every beach in the world. Our concepts of what is possible and impossible would have absolutely no meaning in such a setting.

Keeping this thought in mind, the ending of Atlantis stating that Zeus made a speech in the universe may be a common occurrence in the cosmos. In such an extreme setting as the universe it may not be any more unusual for Zeus to make a speech on a planet in the Pleiades than for our Secretary-General of the United Nations to make a speech on ours. The only rare thing about it might be that his speech was made about our particular planet. It is quite possible, in my view, that the Atlantis drama began on Earth with the Pleiades through Poseidon and ended by the Pleiades through Zeus.

If there is some validity to my theory of Poseidon being from the Pleiades it stands to reason that the beings in that star cluster knew what was happening on Earth since it was they who sent his expedition there. They would keep Earth under surveillance to see how their experiment was progressing. The 'watchers' mentioned so often in the Book of Enoch may have been part of this surveillance from the Pleiades.

If their experiment was failing and causing havoc it would have to be corrected. The last degenerate days of Atlantis and the inferior giants ravishing the Earth in the Book of Enoch, the angels (celestials) in the Book of Revelation wanting to spread seven vials upon the earth (chemical warfare?), etc., may be clues that something was not successful. Leaders such as Zeus back in the Pleiades may have called a meeting with other celestials and decided to nullify the experiment so our young planet could start afresh with a new civilization of mankind—hence, the story of the flood, Noah remaining to propagate the Earth, etc.

H. P. Blavatsky had a theory about the causes that precipitated the Atlantean disaster:

The Atlanteans became a race of magicians. In consequence of this war was declared, the story of which would be too long to narrate; its substance may be found in the disfigured allegories of the race of Cain, the giants, and that of Noah and his righteous family. The conflict came to an end by the submission of Atlantis; which finds its imitation in the story of the Babylonian and Mosaic flood: the giants and magicians . . . and all flesh died . . . and every man. All except Xizuthras and Noah, who are substantially identical with the great father of the Thlinkithians in the Popul Vuh, or the sacred book of the Guatemalans which also tells of his escaping in a large boat, like the Hindu Noah Vaiswasvata.

Manly P. Hall states:

From the Atlanteans the world has received not only the heritage of arts and crafts, philosophies and sciences, ethics and religions, but also the heritage of hate, strife and perversion. The Atlanteans instigated the first war; and it said that all subsequent wars were fought in a fruitless effort to justify the first one and the right and wrong which it caused. Before Atlantis sank, its spiritually illumined initiates, who realized their land was doomed because it departed from the path of light, withdrew from the ill-fated continent. Carrying with them the sacred and secret doctrines, these Atlanteans established themselves in Egypt, where they became its first 'divine' rulers. Nearly all the great cosmological myths forming the foundation of the various sacred books of the world are based on the Atlantis mystery rituals.

In mythology 'The Lightning of Zeus', which obliterated the Titans, sparked a world upheaval and it would have burned up everything had not Atlas ordered Zeus to swamp the flames with a flood. This mythology could be a distorted reflection of cosmic intervention initiated by Zeus from the Pleiades. The union of water with fire in the destruction of the world is repeated in the immemorially ancient literature of humanity, from the Sais hiero-glyphics and Babylonian cuneiforms to the ancient Mexican codices. A similar story is told of one man of the first world being saved from the flood, Deucalion, in the ark, 'lanark', the Babylonian Atrakhasis, the Noah of the Bible and the Book of Enoch.

Plato doesn't mention a flood in Atlantis but breaks his account abruptly leaving us to believe the flood could take place at that point. If that is so there would be strong correlation between Atlantis and other apocryphal texts concerning the flood.

Such catastrophe, confirmed by geologists today, shattered the worldwide civilization of prehistory. Ancient traditions tell of earthquakes, tidal waves, flaming volcanoes, cities swept into the sea, millions of people and animals destroyed and a few frantic survivors fleeing to caves underground, waiting for months in darkness, praying for the sun to return. We may be getting clues in Plato's report of conditions that led up to the flood :

> . . . and thus their wealth did not make them drunk with pride so that they lost control of themselves and went to ruin; rather, in their soberness of mind they clearly saw that all these good things are increased by general amity combined with virtue, whereas the eager pursuit and worship of these goods not only causes the goods themselves to diminish, but makes virtue also to perish with them. As a result, then, of such reasoning and of the continuance of their divine nature all their wealth had grown to such a greatness as we previously described. But when the portion of divinity within them was now becoming faint and weak through being oft times blended with a large measure of mortality, whereas the human temper was becoming dominant, then at length they lost their comeliness, through being unable to bear the burden of their possessions, and became ugly to look upon, in the eyes of him who has the gift of sight; for they had lost the fairest of their goods from the most precious of their parts; but in the eyes of those who have no gift of perceiving what is the truly

happy life, it was then above all that they appeared to be super-latively fair and blessed, filled as they were with lawless ambition and power.

We note now that the Atlanteans have progressed to a high degree of civilization and then morally disintegrated. There is an important clue here in the words "the portion of divinity within them". This could refer to their celestial heritage, being descendants of Taurus through Poseidon. This portion diminishes through time on Earth and human frailty sets in.

This may have been further compounded in other parts of the world by the fact that the other giants who accompanied Poseidon from Taurus imparted evil to earth people. The Taurus space-men had mated with earth women in the same way Poseidon did with Cleito, but in many cases it produced an inferior giant with enormous spiritual powers from space and the common lusts of the Earth. The Book of Enoch may be revealing this truth to us. The following passage has parallels with the preceding Atlantis passage :

IX. 6 "Thou seest what Azazel hath done taught all unrighteousness on earth and revealed the eternal secrets which were (preserved) in heaven, which men were striving to learn."
7. "And Semjaza, to whom Thou hast given authority to bear rule over his associates."
8. "And they have gone to the daughters of men upon the earth and have slept with the women and have defiled themselves, and revealed to them all kinds of sins."
9. "And the women have borne giants and the whole earth has thereby been filled with blood and unrighteousness."
10. "And, now, behold, the souls of those who have died are crying and making their suit to the gates of heaven, and their lamentations have ascended."

These then could be the conditions that led up to the flood and it may be at this point that the Egyptian priests introduced their mysterious character Zeus, near the end of their Atlantis account. He is not mentioned as being associated with the Atlanteans throughout the story but through our theory knows

H           113

their situation. We get suspicious at this point that the flood and Zeus are connected: "And Zeus, the god of gods, who reigns by law, inasmuch as he has the gift of perceiving such things, marked how this righteous race was in evil plight, and desired to inflict punishment upon them, to the end that when chastised they might strike a truer note."

Mythologists doubt the reality of Osiris, Athene, Zeus and Poseidon. They claim these gods as anthropomorphisms of natural forces humanized by the primitive peoples of antiquity. One should not rest on that until the full origins of the Atlantis Egyptian account are known, including who wrote it and what universal dimensions they were connected to. Plato's message from the priests gives nothing to indicate that Zeus is a mythical character in any way. Like Poseidon the account treats him as a real entity only with higher rank. In our twentieth century semantics of gods and spacemen he has higher rank over the other cosmonauts or gods. Zeus and Poseidon may be only a small part of the many expressions of man in the universe. The ancient words "the proper study of mankind is man" may one day be changed to "the proper study of mankind is man in the cosmos".

The ending mentions the strange location in which the celestials hold their meeting in order to discuss the fate of the Atlanteans and their empire back on earth. It appears to have taken place in some sort of 'cosmic' United Nations centre where all the leading members of galactic federations converge. Taken literally it appears that these extraterrestrials knew the entire universe, as "the abode stood in its centre and that it had visions of all the things that partake of generation", and that would have to include the planet Earth. A mind-boggling concept to any present-day astronomer knowing the incredible enormity of the universe. A delight to any science-fiction writer. Our imaginations are expanded further when we are asked to believe that the supreme of all celestials in creation, Zeus, the god of gods, gave a speech in the centre of the universe itself concerning our tiny planet caught in the smoky rim of the Milky Way.

If this seems too extreme we may able to soften it a little. The ancients referred to the Pleiades as the centre of the universe and it may be somewhere on a planet in this star cluster that Zeus made his speech. I think that Zeus and Poseidon may have been from the same planet in the Pleiades but in the next chapter I present a more elaborate theory pertaining to quasars and superior beings in the universe. I found this necessary to defend Plato's exact words in the ending of his report, although I personally believe the Poseidon–Zeus–Pleiades theory. The truth of the location of Zeus may lie in a poem by Aratos describing the Pleiades: ". . . seven paths aloft men say they take, yet six alone are viewed by mortal eyes. From Zeus' abode no star unknown is lost since first from birth we hear, but thus the tale is told. . . ."

Before the flood the Book of Enoch may be stating how The Holy and Great One (Zeus?) relayed a message back to earth concerning Noah. It is planned that his seed will be preserved so a new wave of purified mankind will start in the future:

X. 1. "Then said the Most High, the Holy and Great One spake, and sent Uriel to the son of Lamech, and said to him :"
2. "(Go to Noah and) Tell him in my name 'Hide thyself' and reveal to him the end that is approaching, that the whole earth will be destroyed, and a deluge is about to come upon the whole earth and will destroy all that is on it."
3. "And now instruct him that he may escape and his seed may be preserved for all the generations of the world."

The Book of Enoch gives us a description of the flood itself. In this passage, Noah is referred to as being born a bull and become a man. Perhaps this means that he was born in the Pleiades and then lived as a man on earth. And we note here that three other bulls (Taurus beings?) join him in the vessel. If they were the sole survivors of the flood, we could all be descendants of the Pleiades through Noah :

LXXXIX. 1. "And one of those four went to that white bull and instructed him in a secret, without his being terrified : he was born a bull and became a man, and built for himself a great vessel and they were covered in."

2. "And I saw again, and behold fountains were opened on the roof, with seven water torrents thereon, and those torrents flowed with much water into an enclosure."

3. "And I saw again, and behold fountains were opened on the surface of that great enclosure, and that water began to swell and rise upon the surface, and I saw that enclosure till all its surface was covered with water."

4. "And the water, the darkness, and mist increased upon it; and as I looked at the height of that enclosure, and was streaming over that enclosure, and it stood upon the earth."

5. "And all the cattle of that enclosure were gathered together until I saw how they sank and were swallowed up and perished in that water."

6. "But that vessel floated on the water, while all the oxen and elephants and camels and asses sank to the bottom with all the animals, so that I could no longer see them and they were not able to escape, (but) perished and sank into the depths."

If the theory of Zeus being a real entity is correct then Plato may have recited the most fantastic ending in all the world's literature. He ends his saga of Poseidon, the Taurus giant, and his descendants with a thrilling scene that may be serving as a magic prism to the cosmos. It was probably after this meeting that the flood on earth took place: "Wherefore he assembled together all the gods into that abode which they honour most, standing as it does at the centre of all the universe, and beholding all things that partake of generation; and when he had assembled them, he spake thus: ..."

# SEVENTEEN

# The Universe Beyond Taurus and Earth

In 1968, the universe revealed mystery and drama when unnatural extraterrestrial radio signals were discovered by scientists at Cambridge University. These signals were from what appears to be another dimension in space, pulsars, and radio astronomers at Arecibo, Parkes, the U.S.S.R. and other countries all study this strange phenomenon. Nothing in nature gives a controlled appearance and it is the strange precision of the pulsars that has mystified scientists.

Cambridge scientists discovered four sources of pulsar signals, calculated to be coming from pulsars approximately 200 light years from earth, and within our galaxy. These cosmodynamic lighthouses send signals that arrive in pulses, one exactly every 1·3372795 seconds for a period of one minute; suddenly they vanish for 3–4 minutes; reappear for one minute; and keep repeating the same cycle. The accuracy of the repetition is of far greater precision and consistency than could be achieved with the world's finest electronic equipment. The precision of the pulsars is one every 1·3372795 seconds, with accuracy of one point in 100,000,000. Such accuracy is equal to atomic clocks.

On 15 June 1968, the fifth pulsar was discovered by U.S. radio astronomers operating a radio telescope at the National Radio Astronomy Observatory in Greenbank, West Virginia. This pulsar designated HP 1506 emits one pulse every 0·7397 seconds, and has an accuracy within 1/10,000 of a second. Another—

PSR 0833—pulses extremely rapidly every 0·089 seconds, the fastest at 0·033 seconds. Many new pulsars were discovered, and by mid 1973, 100 had been catalogued.

However even further contrivance was noted in November 1971, reminding one of the ending of Atlantis, describing Zeus and his galactic federation with other gods. A dramatically unusual pulsar was discovered in the Milky Way's northern constellation Hercules—a puzzling X-ray source that pulses every 1·24 seconds for nine days then instantly turns off for twenty-seven days, recommencing the same cycle indefinitely. Dr Frank Drake of Cornell University said about the Hercules pulsar: "This discovery is every bit as bewildering as the finding of the first pulsar five years ago. There is no known reason why a star should disappear and then reappear at such regular and predictable times."*

Even more extreme is a star pulsating near the edge of the Milky Way that could date back 45 billion years, which would make it four times older than the rest of the universe.

The star in question was found four years ago by Britain's Jodrell Bank Observatory and given the unromantic name of JP-1953. The J stands for Jodrell Bank, the P for pulsar and the numbers for the star's co-ordinates in the sky.

JP-1953 lies about 1,000 light years away near the southern edge of the constellation Cygnus, the Swan. The star gives out a radio pulse once every four-tenths of a second and has not deviated from that pulse in the last three years, making it different from the thirty-nine other pulsars in the heavens that have been clocked by the world's largest radio telescope at Arecibo.

"All the other pulsars are spinning down, slowing up if you will," said Cornell's Dr Drake in the *Winnipeg Free Press,* 27 November 1974, "Not this one. We can detect no spin-down in this pulsar, making it clearly a very different beast."

Pulsars are formed out of the leftovers of an exploding star,

* The opening section of this chapter is derived in substance from Robin Collyns's *Did Spacemen Colonize the Earth?* (Pelham Books, London)

literally giving the star a second life. When first formed, pulsars may spin as often as 1,000 times a second, sending beams of light and radio waves across space like lighthouses in the sky. Like cosmic clocks, pulsars in the heavens are winding down and losing a little of their spin each year. This allows astronomers to make what they feel are reasonably accurate estimates of the lifetimes of pulsars.

The Arecibo Observatory puts thirty-nine out of the forty pulsars it has clocked into an age bracket of between 10 and 100 million years. None is older than 100 million years. The thirty-nine stars are spinning down at what Dr Drake calls a "nice reasonable way" for pulsars to behave.

Not the pulsar in Cygnus. No spindown has been detected, even though Arecibo has timed its pulse once a week for the last three years. "We've said O.K., if it's not spinning down, then the pulse should arrive at 12 : 00 in the afternoon, plus 43 minutes and 10 : 35 seconds a year from now," Dr Drake said, "And you wait a year, and the pulse comes back, right on time." In calculating the age of the pulsar in Cygnus, Dr Drake said the youngest it can be is 5 billion years. Its upper limit is 45 billion years. The calculations suggest that the 45 billion year age is more likely than the 5 billion years.

Dr Drake said that everybody at Arecibo is mystified as to what the star really is. He speculates about the 45 billion year age almost in disbelief, then admits he has few working alternatives. "One other thing it can be is an intelligent civilization attempting to communicate with other worlds," Dr Drake said. "Because everybody has said that's how you'd mark yourself. You do something that can't be done in nature. You make the pulse rate of a nearby pulsar exactly right, not deviating in the least year after year."

Astronomers endeavoured to discover natural causes for the unusual behaviour of pulsars, but as soon as the theories were published, the pulsars exhibited new or different characteristics. The *New York Post* said : "Prof. Alan Barret of the Massachusetts Institute of Technology has wondered out loud if these signals could be part of a vast interstellar communications network on which we have stumbled."

In adding to his remarks we wonder if our astronomers are not stumbling into a theory with their massive telescopes that was already contained in a few short sentences pertaining to Zeus at the end of Atlantis. Our ancient literature may be as valuable as our latest astronomical discoveries. It has been suggested that these pulsars are powerful navigation beacons for interstellar convoys so that captains of spaceships do not get lost in the oceans of space. Perhaps the ships come from a common centre, the centre mentioned at the end of Atlantis—"standing as it does in the centre of all the universe, and beholding all things that partake of generation".

Even if the ending of Atlantis is myth and the pulsars are a natural force of nature—pulsating, rapidly rotating neutron stars, or a third class of star, it still remains to be seen whether or not they were artificially created.

Anthropologists have deeply ingrained in us the inferior evolutionary forms of man that have preceded us on Earth; but escaping the scrapings and diggings in the mud of this tiny planet may be evolutions of man transcending ourselves throughout the cosmos. Several Soviet scientists believe there may be higher evolutionary beings in cosmic communities who have progressed to such a technological level that they are actually able to manipulate the behaviour of a star. It lies in today's science fiction and tomorrow's truth how this might be done. Celestials may have imploded pulsars—neutron stars with laser beams, to create navigation beacons, lighting the pathways to galactic cities and the mysterious centre of the universe mentioned at the end of Atlantis.

Another case for the suspicion of intelligence behind the synchronized signals of the pulsars is that they incredibly seem to be all the same age—2,000,000 years old. If they were in a cluster one could give credence to them being the same age, but since they are spread throughout our galaxy our imagination is given its severest shock. Another interesting concentration of pulsars is situated along the plane of the galactic equator.

One might be justified in asking which is more incredible: the so long regarded mythical ending of Atlantis or the stark reality of what our telescopes are actually seeing. These theories of the pulsars are in complete harmony with the Atlantis ending of Zeus and superior beings in the universe. One day every word of the Atlantis transmission may prove to be true.

The incredible vast expanse of our physical universe with its myriads of stars overwhelms our imagination; our minds cannot simply comprehend such immensity. In its new meaning, our galaxy and the universe may be composed of billions of ecological systems on planets thriving with infinite forms of life. And through all this runs an invisible undercurrent, the Universal Intelligence (God), creating life on these thousand million, million planets. Some of the intelligent life created may be far superior to ourselves. In fact, the evolution of man in the cosmos may advance to high levels to where the Universal Intelligence could produce a superior being capable of supervising a particular galaxy such as this one or even our universe. Through evolution, the earth was capable of producing its own Secretary General of the United Nations, so it could seem logical that something far more magnificent such as our universe with a larger reserve of nature to draw upon, would be capable of producing a Secretary General of United Galaxies. Perhaps in the twenty-fifth century the ending of Plato's report will be better understood. In the meantime, the suggestion put forward in the last chapter that Zeus made a speech on a planet in the Pleiades, and that Plato is basically correct, may not be so extreme and may be worth tenure until further answers are found.

# EIGHTEEN

# Our Voyage to the Pleiades

BEFORE MAN can think about leaving Earth and visiting other worlds, he must believe that there are other worlds to visit. And through clues of extraterrestrial visitations on his own planet he must know the general location of these worlds. Otherwise his programmes in space will be aimless.

If there is some validity to the connection between the Earth and its celebrated seven stars it may be worth considering to gear our long-range space programme to the Pleiades. Otherwise after exploration of our limited solar system where are we heading? The following is a passage from *The Exploration of Space* by Arthur C. Clarke,* world renowned authority on outer space. Mr Clarke does not mention the Pleiades but theorises on how we can travel beyond our solar system where the realm of these stars lie:

To send a spaceship to the stars, if the time factor is of no importance, requires little more energy than many interplanetary missions. Thus a rocket which left the Earth at a speed of fifteen miles a second would still have eleven miles a second of its original velocity left when it had escaped completely from the Solar System If aimed in the correct direction, it would reach any of the nearer stars (ignoring, for the moment, the fact that the stars themselves are in motion at speeds of several miles a second). The journey to Proxima Centauri would last a trifle more than 70,000 years. Thus although a *very* far-sighted civilisation might consider it worth while sending messages to the nearer stars in the faint hope of getting some sort of reply a few hundred thousand years later, this is hardly what one has in mind when speaking of interstellar travel!

* Reprinted by permission of the author and the authors agents, Scott Meredith Literary Agency, Inc., 845 Third Ave, New York, N.Y. 10022.

Clearly, speeds comparable to the velocity of light will be needed if even the nearest stars are to be reached in a human lifetime. As has already been stated, there are eight stellar systems within ten light-years of the Sun. Given unlimited power, there is no theoretical reason why such speeds should not be obtained : they are, however, as much beyond our reach today as present rocket speeds would have been beyond the attainment of the men who built the first steam-engines. The velocity of light is 670,000,000 m.p.h.—and we have seen how difficult it is to achieve the modest 25,000 m.p.h. or so needed for interplanetary travel. It is obvious that before interstellar travel can enter the realm of serious study, some new method of propulsion, coupled with a source of energy vastly more powerful than anything in sight today, will be required.

It is hardly likely that the rocket will always remain undisputed master of space : its disadvantages are so many and so obvious that if anything better comes along astronauts will seize upon it with considerable joy. Nevertheless it is just possible that some form of rocket propulsion might play a part in taking mankind, literally, to the stars. After the chemical and the atomic rockets will come the electric, or ion, rocket—a device whose outlines can be foreseen even today. It is possible, by appropriate electric and magnetic fields, to accelerate charged particles (ions) to velocities near that of light. A beam of such particles would act as a rocket jet and could produce a thrust—indeed, there is a well-known laboratory experiment to demonstrate this. With ordinary currents and powers the thrust is negligible, but there is no fundamental reason why such a device should not be developed for propulsion, particularly under the conditions prevailing in space.

To attain really high speeds by this means it would be necessary to have an extremely efficient source of nuclear energy : anything like our present atomic power plants would be completely useless. Some means would be required of releasing a large percentage of the energy of matter (not merely the 0·1 per cent we can liberate today) and then transferring it, with negligible losses, to the ion beam. No way is known of doing this, but it does not involve any inherent impossibility. With the *total* annihilation of the 'fuel' —i.e. its complete conversion into energy—we should have the extreme case of a rocket whose 'exhaust' would consist entirely of light, the thrust of which under ordinary circumstances is far too small to be of any importance, though even an electric hand-torch gives an immeasurably small 'kick' when switched on.

123

How fast the rocket itself would travel would depend on the weight of the fuel it carried, although owing to the Theory of Relativity the laws now operating would be more complicated than those explained in Chapter 3. When we allow for this, we find that if we could build a rocket 90 per cent of whose mass consisted of fuel which was converted entirely into radiation, the empty rocket would reach a speed equal to 98 per cent of that of light, or just over 600,000,000 m.p.h. At this speed, it would reach the nearest star in four and three-quarter years. However, we are dealing with such enormous velocities that the period of acceleration (negligible in interplanetary flight) must now be considered, and this would increase the time of transit by a considerable factor. Indeed, on the 'shorter' ( ! ) interstellar flights it would be necessary to start decelerating again well before the speed of light had been approached.

As is now well known, at velocities approaching that of light some very peculiar things begin to happen. These were pointed out by Einstein when he formulated the Special Theory of Relativity, and they have since been demonstrated experimentally in certain cases. The effects which concern us here involve the mass of an interstellar spaceship, and the 'time-scale' of its occupants.

The mass of a body increases with its speed. The effect is immeasurably small at ordinary velocities, and is still negligible at speeds of many thousand miles a second. But it becomes all-important as one nears the velocity of light, and at that speed the mass of any object would become infinite. This, of course, is merely another way of saying that the velocity of light can be approached as closely as one pleases but can never be actually attained. (Like the absolute zero of temperature.)

In addition to the increase of mass, there is also what might be called a 'stretching' of time. If one could 'compare' a minute, as observed in the spaceship, with one on Earth, it would appear to be longer. Again the effect is very small at ordinary speeds but becomes enormous as one nears the velocity of light. At this limiting speed, in fact, time would appear to stand still.

It will be seen that this relativity effect is working in the right direction, as far as the interstellar travellers are concerned. From their point of view, it reduces the duration of the voyage. However, it is important to realise that this time-contraction only becomes really significant at speeds greater than half that of light —i.e. over 300,000,000 m.p.h.

To take an actual example consider the spaceship mentioned

on page 176, which, by converting 90 per cent of its mass into radiation, reached a speed equal to 98 per cent that of light. Suppose it left Earth at an acceleration of two gravities and maintained this until it had reached its final speed. Then, from the viewpoint of the crew, the period of acceleration would have lasted just over a year. But from the viewpoint of an observer on Earth, the ship would have been accelerating for five and a half years!

Dr. Sänger, the noted German rocket expert, has made some calculations for an even more extreme case, purely as a matter of theoretical interest. He considers a spaceship *circumnavigating the Cosmos*—assuming that this represents a distance of 10,000,000,000 light years. If the ship could achieve 99·999,999,999,999,999,996 per cent of the velocity of light, the crew would imagine that the journey lasted thirty-three years— yet 10,000,000,000 years would have elapsed before they returned to Earth (if it still existed!). Since this feat would require the complete conversion into energy of a mass approaching that of the Moon, Sänger reasonably concluded that it surpasses the limits of what is ever likely to become technically feasible!

Without going to such an extreme case, however, it would seem that stars up to twenty or thirty light-years away could, in theory, be reached within a single human lifetime. The idea does not involve any mathematical or physical impossibilities, and the feat would not require too enormous amounts of fuel *if* the total conversion of mass into energy could be achieved. Although, at the moment, we have no idea how this might be done, it must be remembered that nuclear physics is still in its infancy.

Since several decades of travelling through space would be an ordeal even to the most enthusiastic astronauts, one cannot help wondering if medical science might come to the rescue with some form of suspended animation—another theoretical possibility still outside the range of present achievement. If this became practicable, it might extend the range of space-flight almost indefinitely— assuming that travellers could be found willing to return to Earth perhaps generations after their departure, when everyone they had ever known was dead and society itself might have changed out of all recognition.

Bernal, in the book already mentioned, has suggested that mobile artificial worlds, carrying whole populations on journeys which might last for centuries, may be used for interstellar travel. (In this sense, of course, we on this planet are interstellar voyagers already—though our journey is involuntary and we know neither its destination nor its beginning.) Such dirigible planetoids might travel at a few per cent of the velocity of light : there would be no appreciable time contraction at such speeds and after a trip round the nearer stars the fifth or tenth grandchildren of those who began the journey would return to Earth. It is, however, difficult to see how a major fraction of the Cosmos could ever be explored by this means, since it would take some millions of years to travel from one end of the Galaxy to the other.

Even if one grants the existence of the necessary source of power, it may be asked if these enormous speeds are physically realisable owing to the existence of interstellar gas as well as of solid meteoric material in space. As far as the latter is concerned, calculations show that the danger is negligible, and it does not seem that interstellar hydrogen would be a menace except possibly at speeds not far short of that of light, when it might be necessary to consider some form of shielding.

The discovery of other forms of propulsion, not depending on the rocket principle, would not materially affect the above arguments. Perhaps one day, when we have learned something about gravitation and the structure of space, we may be able to produce one of the 'space-drives' so beloved of science-fiction writers. These drives, for the benefit of anyone unacquainted with contemporary mythology, have the great advantage that, since the force they produce acts uniformly on every atom inside the spaceship, accelerations of any magnitude can be produced with no strain on the passengers. Even if the ship were accelerating at a thousand gravities, the occupants would still feel weightless.

There is nothing inherently absurd about this idea : in fact, a gravitational field produces precisely this effect. If one were falling freely towards Jupiter not far outside the planet's atmosphere, one would be accelerating at $2\frac{1}{2}$ gravities yet would be completely weightless. To take an even more extreme case, the very dense dwarf star Sirius B has a surface gravity at least 20,000 times as intense as the Earth's. Falling in such a field one would be accelerating more rapidly than a shell while it was being fired from a gun, but there would be no feeling of strain whatsoever.

If we can ever generate the equivalent of a controlled gravitational field we shall certainly have a very effective drive for spaceships—one which, combined with an appropriate source of energy, might enable speeds near that of light to be reached after relatively brief periods of acceleration. It would not, however, help us to circumvent the restrictions set by the Theory of Relativity. As far as any fact can be experimentally established, it seems certain that no material body can ever travel faster than light. This limit is a fundamental one, of a completely different character from the so-called 'sonic barrier' which once seemed an obstacle to high-speed flight. There was never any doubt that one could fly faster than sound, *given sufficient energy* : the only problem was to obtain this energy, and like all purely technical problems this was eventually solved. But even the disintegration of all the matter in the Universe would not provide enough energy to enable a space-ship to reach the speed of light.

It appears, therefore, that when astronautical techniques have reached the limits set by the laws of Nature (and we must assume that eventually these limits *will* be reached, even though we are very far from them today) it will be possible to send expeditions to the nearer stars and for them to return within ten or twenty years—though the period of elapsed time might be considerably less to the travellers themselves.

To imagine any long-range exploration of the Universe we have to assume voyages lasting many centuries, or even millions of years. Such voyages could be possible only if whole generations were willing to exile themselves in space. This would not necessarily be a great hardship when one considers that a mobile planetoid would probably be a good deal larger—and would have incomparably greater facilities in every respect—than the State of Athens, in which small area it may be remembered, a surprising number of men led remarkably fruitful lives.

It is, perhaps, worth pointing out that our present views on the subject of interstellar flight are conditioned by the span of human life. There is no reason whatsoever to suppose that this will always be less than a century. When we reach the stars, the achievement may be due as much to medicine as to physics. As Man's expectation of life increases, so a greater and greater volume of space will become accessible to exploration.

Before closing this chapter we must deal with two questions which any discussion of interstellar travel inevitably raises. In the first place, despite the categorical remarks made a few pages ago, can we be *absolutely* certain that the speed of light will never be surpassed? The Theory of Relativity is, after all, only a theory. May it not one day be modified, just as it modified Newton's law of gravitation, which had remained inviolate for centuries and was generally regarded as being absolutely correct?

Any attempt to answer this question would lead into the deep waters of philosophy, and would involve such ideas as the fundamental structure of space and time. It is doubtful if anyone alive today could contribute much of real value to such a discussion : the verdict must be left to the future. At the moment we can only say that the idea of speeds greater than light still belongs to that nebulous and faintly disreputable no-man's-land where may be found the Fourth Dimension, telepathy, and Dr Rhine's disturbing experiments in para-physics.

In commenting on these quotes by Arthur C. Clarke we see there may be possibilities of one day going to the Pleiades but there will have to be new concepts and inventions we are still not fully aware of. Time seems to be the first factor and energy second. Speeds beyond the velocity of light will be needed if the Pleiades are to be reached in the framework of a human lifetime. At the speed of light four centuries would be required to reach the Pleiades and something such as Mr Clarke's suggestion of medical science may have to aid such an event.

For all we know these methods may have already been used by others such as Poseidon if you accept the theory that he visited us from the Pleiades. His visitation may have been only a small part of our surveillance from space. Countless times in geological history expedition ships may have winged down from celestial empires, passed through the clouds of Earth, and left again with records of steaming seas, the first primitive amphibians, slithering on our beaches, and much later still, the giant dinosaurs. And, even now, there may be fleets of survey ships diligently charting and recharting the universe. Another chapter suggests the quasars are beacons for them. The record of extraterrestrial visitors extends from the soaring vimanas of ancient India to the 'flying saucers' of today.

Even if we never reach the Pleiades by our own efforts, in the millions of years that lie ahead it may be possible that they would pay a return visit. Isolationism may be against the natural laws of the universe and the reason Poseidon and the Taurus giants once visited us. Planets in the Pleiades may still contain records of their Earth visitations in the same way our planet seems to contain apocryphal texts of such activity. If these theories are correct our visit to the Pleiades would put us in a slightly passive role since we would not be the discoverers but the discovered.

Our technological civilization is becoming incomprehensible even to ourselves in our own time, and almost totally unimagined to others a generation ago. We are now on the threshold of space and take our complex society for granted. One day we may be part of an inter-galactic federation involving the Pleiades which would be so much a part of ourselves that we would scarcely realize its presence. The important factor is, of course, the motive. What will the motives be which will drive men out into space, and send them to the worlds of the Pleiades—worlds that may be hostile to human life?

One day we may have to pioneer our solar system and the Pleiades because of limited resources on our planet. These worlds may have to be colonized because of our severe demographic problem. Also the conquest of space could release our atomic power, dangerously accumulating in the narrow confines of Earth. This constructive use of our atomic energy sending us to the stars could also release our aggressive and pioneering instincts and put them to good use in the challenges of space. Otherwise, the infinite human mind, confined to the finite area of Earth, might decay and bring about total destruction.

Conversely, if our theories are correct we can see by our history that the arrival of the Taurus giants on Earth led to the partial destruction of our planet. A visit to their regions may cause similar chaos. It may be wiser to focus our attention here and make our world a better place to live. However, if there is any truth to Plato's recital the first days of Atlantis seemed to flourish on a high moral plane under the cosmic influence of Poseidon. Our voyage to the Pleiades may put us in contact with highly evolved creatures such as him. And that in itself would be worth the trip.

The prospect of meeting higher evolutionary forms of man may be one of the strongest motivations for space travel in the future. I believe it is closely coming to the point when our aloneness in the Universe should no longer be a supreme question of

I                                   129

philosophy. Contemporary writers seem to be finding new revelations through our history that the world is anthropologically connected to other worlds. The future may demand a surge of further answers and only through space travel will they be obtained. One day the direction of that space travel may be the Pleiades.

# NINETEEN

# Our Discoveries in the Pleiades

IN RECENT YEARS the development of new astronomical instruments leading to a landing on Mars has given us much more accurate information about other planets in our solar system. Through our precise knowledge of conditions on Earth, our direct contact with the moon and Mars, we are starting to build a broad base for scientific discussion of life in the cosmos. From the continuing of these advances we may one day learn more about life in the Pleiades in the same way we are learning about our Earth and solar system.

Even if our probes into our solar system are negative it will increase our sense of perspective, and our neighbouring planets will serve as stepping stones to broader areas of interest. The Pleiades are a raft in our galaxy as both float for ever in the rivers of the universe. Our Mars landing is a great step in conquering that raft and bringing the secrets of the Pleiades back to Earth.

For all practical purposes the Earth has been linked to its sun and solar system but our ties may not be so much with our solar system as they are with the Pleiades. In the vast canopy of heaven, the universe would mix her species in much more dramatic ways than the limited life welding of a solar system. The Pleiades may be the centre of human life in our galaxy and not our solar system. Our solar system has been taken as an extreme focal point, and one day science will physically transcend this through spinning payloads gliding beyond its domains. More than fifty years ago, the Russian pioneer space scientist Tsiolkokovski wrote the following words : "The earth is the cradle of the mind—but you can not live in the cradle forever."

Now as we enter the second decade of the space age we can still look further in the future. The Earth is our cradle which we are about to leave, and the solar system may be our kindergarten; the Pleiades our adolescence; our galaxy and beyond our adulthood. In the meantime, we are left with a great deal of telescopic scanning and block building from our earthly clues pertaining to further celestial systems.

If anything, astronomy teaches men humility. We know the myriads of suns in the Pleiades may be important members of vast families of planets and perhaps those planets have further ties with us. Carl Sagan has calculated that in our Milky Way galaxy, one planet in approximately two thousand is nearly a duplicate of earth. If this is so, and our theories of Poseidon are correct, it may not be unreasonable to conclude that we have a sister planet in the Pleiades—a similar structure to Earth that gave birth to Poseidon. If such a world exists in the Pleiades we would be able to step out of our expedition ships, take deep breaths of oxygen-rich air, look up at a blue sky, and exert ourselves with the same gravitational pull we felt at home. Poseidon may have been able to do exactly that when he landed on Earth.

Our search for Poseidon's birthplace may also be the planet that once spawned a United Nations system of which Zeus was Secretary General thousands of years before he dissolved into mythology on Earth. This planet, if it still exists, would have the remnants of many past nations that rose to a degree of civilization capable of sending Poseidon's expedition to Earth. It probably contained or contains further sources of many of our institutions mentioned in a previous chapter. The origins of these teachings may be on this planet or elsewhere in the universe. Capable of supporting forms of human life, it was or is vegetated, containing many animals similar to Earth. Like man, various animals on our planet are probably scattered throughout the cosmos. In particular, the bull which may have become a symbol of the Taurus constellation throughout our galaxy.

Our landing on such a planet could be an exhilarating experience. Colours might become vivid and contrasts sharper. Everything might begin appearing as a work of art, a feast for our eyes. Even inanimate objects might assume a lifelike quality. Our surroundings might be suddenly filled with vitality. We would begin noticing how our sister planet was a closed system, like a comparable working model of Earth itself, recycling all of life's dynamic forces. Sprawled out before us could be a world teeming with life in which we would commence to study, collect and catalogue.

As beautiful as this experience might be, if we met intelligent beings in the Pleiades we would have no guarantee that they would be benign, and contact with them might spark similar conflicts we have had on Earth. If our explorations led us to Poseidon's posterity the cultural shock of direct contact may be too great for us to survive. If they were too far advanced, technologically or spiritually, we may be overwhelmed and subjected to the position of retardates in the presence of supreme universal intelligence and expression in the same way an ape man might be confronted with great cities.

This may not be far-fetched since we see by experiences on our own world that human societies have an almost unbelievable range of behaviour and alien creatures may behave in ways incomprehensible to us such as when the giants were on earth with enormous spiritual powers. Even judging from the examples of our own ecology, where life is based on the same biochemical system, the ingenuity of nature seems unlimited. Life in the Pleiades could fall in the same endless exaggeration. The divine plan of the universe may be infinite expression and creativity. Even so, this wouldn't stop basic patterns running throughout and Poseidon and ourselves may be the general form of man throughout the cosmos.

The Pleiades may have inhabited worlds circling many suns, harbouring higher civilizations of man with cultures beyond our wildest dreams. But it will be a long time before we will meet them and they for the most part probably do not know of our existence although they may have a record of their visitations to Earth. That their civilizations exist may be an opinion of respect since most astronomers today do not heavily entertain the idea that we are alone in the universe. If, however, our theories are incorrect and there is no life in the Pleiades such a negative finding would give us an idea of how life in the universe is distributed and by what conditions it is likely to evolve.

Clues to life past and present in the Pleiades might be the finding on many planets of titanic blocks of stone piled one upon the other similar to the discarded monuments left by the Taurus giants on Earth. Like Earth, many planets may be stamped with the symbol of the Taurus or cosmic bull. Somewhere, or in many places may be recorded the heroic explorations of Poseidon and the story of Atlantis may be a familiar saga to many. Perhaps our galaxy and even the universe has a recorded history—a mass of connecting threads in literary form. The fantastic tale of Poseidon and Atlantis and other numerous accounts may have been passed through various civilizations of the cosmos and the ending pertaining to Zeus would be well known and understood by superior beings who convert orbits of planets and change stars into pulsating quasars for space ships.

The Pleiades themselves may be in an advanced state, transcending our own science fiction. Their societies may hum with connections to remote areas of our galaxy and the universe-societies that are part of an intergalactic federation. There may be noble civilizations where kings, princes, militarists and beautiful women mingle in brilliant societies similar to the Atlantis society initiated by the Pleiades on Earth. In fact, Atlantis may be the floating blueprint for man's civilization throughout the cosmos. God (celestial initiator), king (half celestial) and prince may be a normal social expression of man in the universe as it once was in the Pleiades since it may be a duplicate copy reprinted by Poseidon. Atlantis may have been only a transplant from cosmic cities in the Pleiades surrounded by walls encasing architecture glowing with berylium, silver and orichalcum.

If the theory is accepted that the Pleiades initiated a large part of our civilization, the fair question to ask is who initiated the Pleiades? And of course, the answer to that question is *ad infinitum* because we must ask who in turn initiated that civilization, etc. Planets in the Pleiades may have unusual histories like ours. Wondrous beings outside the Pleiades may have descended and ruled their planets in glorious golden ages or the infusion eventually caused chaos similar to when the giants stayed on Earth too long. This might have caused the Pleiades civilizations to rebel, catastrophes ravaged their planets, the space kings returned to distant galaxies leaving them to build their civilizations again. The biblical flood may be a common occurrence in the cosmos and a great many versions might be recorded in a multitude of sources. One strong case for the Pleiades being colonized from elsewhere is that the cluster is younger than our sun and solar system. They are about 50 million years old and we are about 5 billion giving them less time to evolve solar systems containing civilizations similar to Earth. Nonetheless, a great deal of evolution can take place in 50 million years and if intelligent life exists there they could be a mixture of their own evolution and that of distant regions in space. In the same way our theories have shown that we have been products of both this planet and the cosmos. Also astronomers theorize that life could have evolved faster in the Pleiades than on Earth if certain elements were present such as shallow seas and cosmic radiation. We have a great deal to learn about the infinite combinations that make evolution possible, and therefore should keep an open mind about life in this young cluster of stars.

Although many arguments can be given for life in the Pleiades, it may be that all suns in the Pleiades do not contain planetary systems; those that do may have planets that are either barren or bear no intelligent life as we are finding in our solar system. Those planets capable of life may only contain the remnants of civilizations, since intelligence is the end product of a combination of factors, which unfortunately are compounded by a tendency toward self-destruction. This factor could make intelligence a rare find in the Pleiades. Still, if we conservatively estimated one planet in ten stars in the Pleiades contained a planet similar to our own we would have the evolution of twenty-five global civilizations in which to observe. If such planets were found, it may not be normal to find them all living at the same time, cosmically speaking. We see examples of that in a smaller way on our own planet. Some people in the jungles of Africa, South America and Australia are still in the Stone Age of development, while many other peoples in the rest of the world still cling to past centuries. On a broader scale entire planets containing life in various evolutionary stages may be scattered throughout the Pleiades. One day we may carry out Universal Law and be the Atlanteans initiating some of these worlds to a higher degree of civilization in the same way Atlantis initiated Earth. This might be a more expansive role than remaining isolated in space that might lead to the stagnation of science and spiritual sterility which could be further advanced in the marvellous wonder of the cosmos. Even if we desired isolationism, such events as our landing on Mars may be setting our interstellar destiny. However, no one knows the ending of a play until it is over. We will have to wait and see.

Primitive men in the cosmos are probably shielded from contact and communication with people different from themselves through fear, taboo and distance. Gradually, it may be they become able to absorb and benefit from communication with other tribes, races and cosmic initiators. Such contact has probably led to wars and annihilation but some of this communication may have led to intermarriage, not only of people (even cosmic entities such as Poseidon and Cleito), but languages, culture and art. Rapid communication and interchange of ideas, cultures and crafts between peoples once isolated by language and land barriers has resulted in organizations on our own planet such as the United Nations. The Earth may be a microcosm of the macrocosm. Everything on Earth may be a smaller version of what happens in the universe. Our probings in space may one day lead to our contacting the Pleiades, producing an extension of our societies and events which is totally beyond our present comprehension.

In past centuries such a consideration would be relegated by orthodox science as 'occult gibberish' even though such ancient astronomers as Anaxagoras had entertained the idea of life in the cosmos and Giordano expounded such a belief. Formal religion considered such ideas as being heretical and detracting from the special eminence given earthmen as the sole survivor in the entire universe. Even in more modern times such notions were left to science fiction, and any thought about them was considered beneath the dignity of the scientific world.

The space age has transformed this attitude. The prominence of celestial bodies in scientific enquiry has usurped the importance of the Earth not only astronomically but for other sciences studying the heavens as well. Biology and all life sciences are now showing an intense interest in the probability of life in our solar system and its existence in remote worlds and galaxies thousands of light years distant from our little cosmic speck, Earth. Focusing these activities into the constellation of Taurus may one day reveal life in the Pleiades.

Many and beautiful are the star clusters that drift like floating palaces in the heavenly pathways of our galaxy. Most for the present lie beyond our reach, probably knowing nothing of our existence. The Pleiades may not be one of these : its magnificence and beauty may be of a different order. Perhaps it holds countless worlds—superior worlds that have spawned celestials like Poseidon and sent them to our world—worlds that are connected to our past and our future.

## TWENTY

# Plato: The Pleiades Document

WE HAVE PRESENTED evidence that Atlantis was somewhere near Gibraltar in the North African regions and Tarshish in Spain. But, unfortunately, Atlantis has not been found and until it is discovered all works pertaining to it will only be conjecture, including our Pleiades theory.

However, it is hoped that this theory has served as an aid to show the credence of the Egyptian account which the greatest minds in Greece took seriously. Physical science may not be able to provide all the answers concerning the origins of man and our literature may be offering many clues to the mysteries that lie in the mists of creation. It may be centuries before the Atlantis enigma is solved and viewed in its full perspective in the universe. Nonetheless, a beginning can be made to move Atlantis out of the realm of mythology if the following points are worthy of consideration:

1. The account is meant to be viewed in the perspective of our planet and the universe because Plato placed it in *Timaeus* which is a work of the universe. The very first lines are in accord with this and tell of celestials (gods) who divided our planet amongst themselves.

2. The semantic meaning of Plato's word 'god' as applied to Poseidon means celestial. Poseidon is not mythical in any way but a giant from space. The statue in the temple symbolizes his stature and his inter-galactic voyage.

3. He isolated an earth woman and through genetic engineering produced the unnatural combination of five sets of male twins.

138

These half-celestials produced our first concept of royalty on this planet.

4. Atlantis was at Tarshish, named after the Taurus constellation, the origins of Poseidon. It was just outside the Pillars of Heracles with the true continent of the Americas lying beyond. It ignited the Mediterranean civilization of which Crete is still a reflection of this prehistory.

5. The ceremony involving a bull denotes the 'cosmic bull of Taurus', and his blood running down the inscriptions signifies the importance of sacred laws from that constellation handed down to Earth. The Pleiades are in this constellation and could be the origins of Poseidon.

6. The source of the story is Plato via Egypt. The origins of the story are not known and may have been handed down to us by celestials who had knowledge of the vast domains of the universe. The incredible ending might mean that the Pleiades had initiated Atlantis through Poseidon and ended it through Zeus. They that created it destroyed it.

The following is a copy of the Atlantis account that one day may be referred to as 'The Pleiades Document'. It is a marvellous piece of writing :

Like as we previously stated concerning the allotments of the Gods, that they portioned out the whole earth, here into larger allotments and there into smaller, and provided for themselves shrines and sacrifices, even so Poseidon took for his allotment the island of Atlantis and settled therein the children whom he had begotten of a mortal woman in a region of the island of the following description. Bordering on the sea and extending through the centre of the whole island there was a plain, which is said to have been the fairest of all plains and highly fertile; and, moreover, near the plain, over against its centre, at a distance of about 50 stades, there stood a mountain that was low on all sides. Thereon dwelt one of the natives originally sprung from the earth, Evenor by name, with his wife Leucippe; and they had for offspring an only-begotten daughter, Cleito. And when this damsel was now come to marriageable age, her mother died and also her father; and Poseidon being smitten with desire for her, wedded her; and to make the hill whereon she dwelt impregnable he broke it off all round about; and he made circular belts of sea and land enclosing one another alternately, some greater, some smaller, two being of land and three of sea, which he carved as it were out of the midst of the island; and these belts were at even distances on all sides, so as to be impassable for man; for at that time neither ships nor sailing were as yet in existence. And Poseidon himself set in order with ease, as a god would, the central island, bringing up from beneath the earth two springs of waters, the one flowing warm from its source, the other cold, and producing out of the earth all kinds of food in plenty. And he begat five pairs of twin sons and reared them up; and when he had divided all the island of Atlantis into ten portions, he assigned to the first-born of the eldest sons, his mother's dwelling and the allotment surrounding it, which was the largest and best; and him he appointed to be king over the rest, and the others to be rulers, granting to each the rule over many men and a large tract of country. And to all of them he gave names, giving to him that was eldest and king the name after which the whole island was called and the sea spoken of as the Atlantic, because the first king who then reigned had the name of Atlas. And the name of his younger twin-brother, who had for his portion the extremity of the island near the pillars of Heracles up to the part of the country now called Gadeira after the name of that region, was Eumelus in Greek, but in the native tongue Gadeirus, —which fact may have given its title to the country. And of the pair that were born next he called the one Ampheres and the other Evaemon; and of the third pair the elder was named Mneseus and the younger Autochthon; and of the fourth pair, he called the first Elasippus and the second Mestor; and of the fifth pair, Azaes was the name given to the elder, and Diaprepes to the second. So all these, themselves and their descendants, dwelt for many generations bearing rule over many other islands throughout the sea and holding sway besides, as was previously stated, over the Mediterranean peoples as far as Egypt and Tuscany.

Now a large family of distinguished sons sprang from Atlas; but it was the eldest, who as king, always passed on the sceptre to the eldest of his sons, and thus they preserved the sovereignty for many generations; and the wealth they possessed was so immense that the like had never been seen before in any royal house nor will ever easily be seen again; and they were provided with everything of which provision was needed either in the city or throughout the rest of the country. For because of their head-ship they had a large supply of imports from abroad, and the island itself furnished most of the requirements of daily life,—metals, to begin with, both the hard kind and the fusible kind, which are extracted by mining, and also that kind which is now known only by name but was more than a name then, there being mines of it in many places of the island,—I mean 'orichalcum' which was the most precious of the metals then known, except gold. It brought forth also in abundance all the timbers that a forest provides for the labours of carpenters; and of animals it produced a sufficiency, both of tame and wild. Moreover, it con-tained a very large stock of elephants; for there was an ample food-supply not only for all the other animals which haunt the marshes and lakes and rivers, or the mountains or the plains, but likewise also for this animal, which of its nature is the largest and most voracious. And in addition to all this, it produced and brought to perfection all those sweet-scented stuffs which the earth produces now, whether made of roots or herbs or trees, or of liquid gums derived from flowers or fruits. The cultivated fruit also, and the dry, which serves us for nutriment, and all the other kinds that we use for our meals—the various species of which are com-prehended under the name 'vegetables',—and all the produce of trees which affords liquid and solid food and unguents, and the fruit of the orchard-trees, so hard to store, which is grown for the sake of amusement and pleasure, and all the after-dinner fruits that we serve up as welcome remedies for the sufferer from repletion,—all these that hallowed island, as it lay then beneath the sun, produced in marvellous beauty and endless abundance. And thus, receiving from the earth all these products, they fur-nished forth their temples and royal dwellings, their harbours and their docks, and all the rest of their country, ordering all in the fashion following.

First of all they bridged over the circles of sea which surrounded the ancient metropolis, making thereby a road towards and from the royal palace. And they had built the palace at the very beginning where the settlement was first made by their God and their ancestors; and as each king received it from his predecessor, he added to its adornment and did all he could to surpass the king before him, until finally they made of it an abode amazing to behold for the magnitude and beauty of its workmanship. For, beginning at the sea, they bored a channel right through to the outermost circle, which was three plethra in breadth, one hundred feet in depth, and fifty stades in length; and thus they made the entrance to it from the sea like that to a harbour by opening out a mouth large enough for the greatest ships to sail through. Moreover, through the circles of land, which divided those of sea, over against the bridges they opened out a channel leading from circle to circle, large enough to give passage to a single trireme; and this they roofed over above so that the sea-way was subterranean; for the lips of the land-circles were raised a sufficient height above the level of the sea. The greatest of the circles into which a boring was made for the sea was three stades in breadth, and the circle of land next to it was of equal breadth; and of the second pair of circles that of water was two stades in breadth and that of dry land equal again to the preceding one of water; and the circle which ran round the central island itself was of a stade's breadth. And this island, wherein stood the royal palace, was of five stades in diameter. Now the island and the circles and the bridge, which was a plethrum in breadth, they encompassed round about, on this side and on that, with a wall of stone; and upon the bridges on each side, over against the passages for the sea, they erected towers and gates. And the stone they quarried beneath the central island all round, and from beneath the outer and inner circles, some of it being white, some black and some red; and while quarrying it they constructed two inner docks hollowed out and roofed over by the native rock. And of the buildings some they framed of one simple colour, in others they wove a pattern of many colours by blending the stones for the sake of ornament so as to confer upon the buildings a natural charm. And they covered with brass, as though with a plaster, all the circumference of the wall which surrounded the outermost circle; and that of the inner one they coated with tin; and that which encompassed the acropolis itself with orichalcum which sparkled like fire.

The royal palace within the acropolis was arranged in this manner. In the centre there stood a temple sacred to Cleito and Poseidon, which was reserved as holy ground, and encircled with a wall of gold; this being the very spot where at the beginning they had generated and brought to birth the family of the ten royal lines. Thither also they brought year by year from all the ten allotments their seasonable offerings to do sacrifice to each of those princes. And the temple of Poseidon himself was a stade in length, three plethra in breadth, and of a height which appeared symmetrical therewith; and there was something of the barbaric in its appearance. All the exterior of the temple they coated with silver, save only the pinnacles, and these they coated with gold. As to the interior, they made the roof all of ivory in appearance, variegated with gold and silver and orichalcum, and all the rest of the walls and pillars and floors they covered with orichalcum. And they placed therein golden statues, one being that of the God standing on a chariot and driving six winged steeds, his own figure so tall as to touch the ridge of the roof, and round about him a hundred Nereids on dolphins (for that was the number of them as men then believed); and it contained also many other images, the votive offerings of private men. And outside, round about the temple, there stood images in gold of all the princes, both themselves and their wives, as many as were descended from the ten kings, together with many other votive offerings both of the kings and of private persons not only from the State itself but also from all the foreign peoples over whom they ruled. And the altar, in respect of its size and its workmanship, harmonised with its surroundings; and the royal palace likewise was such as befitted the greatness of the kingdom, and equally befitted the splendour of the temples.

The springs they made use of, one kind being of cold, another of warm water, were of abundant volume, and each kind was wonderfully well adapted for use because of the natural taste and excellence of its waters; and these they surrounded with buildings and with plantations of trees such as suited the waters; and, moreover, they set reservoirs round about, some under the open sky, and others under cover to supply hot baths in the winter; they put separate baths for the kings and for the private citizens, besides others for women, and others again for horses and all other beasts of burden, fitting out each in an appropriate manner. And the outflowing water they conducted to the sacred grove of Poseidon, which contained trees of all kinds that were of marvellous beauty and height because of the richness of the soil; and by means of channels they led the water to the outer circles over against the bridges. And there they had constructed many temples for gods, and many gardens and many exercising grounds, some for men and some set apart for horses, in each of the circular belts of island; and besides the rest they had in the centre of the large island a racecourse laid out for horses, which was a stade in width, while as to length, a strip which ran round the whole circumference was reserved for equestrian contests. And round about it, on this side and on that, were barracks for the

143

greater part of the spearmen; but the guard-house of the more trusty of them was posted in the smaller circle, which was nearer the acropolis; while those who were the most trustworthy of all had dwellings granted to them within the acropolis round about the persons of the kings.

And the shipyards were full of triremes and all the tackling that belongs to triremes, and they were all amply equipped.

Such then was the state of things round about the abode of the kings. And after crossing the three outer harbours one found a wall which began at the sea and ran round in a circle, at a uniform distance of fifty stades from the largest circle and harbour, and its ends converged at the seaward mouth of the channel. The whole of this wall had numerous houses built on to it, set close together; while the sea-way and the largest harbour were filled with ships and merchants coming from all quarters, which by reason of their multitude caused clamour and tumult of every description and an unceasing din night and day.

Now as regards the city and the environs of the ancient dwelling we have now wellnigh completed the description as it was originally given. We must endeavour next to repeat the account of the rest of the country, what its natural character was, and in what fashion it was ordered. In the first place, then, according to the account, the whole region rose sheer out of the sea to a great height, but the part about the city was all a smooth plain, enclosing it round about, and being itself encircled by mountains which stretched as far as to the sea; and this plain had a level surface and was as a whole rectangular in shape, being 3,000 stades long on either side and 2,000 stades wide at its centre, reckoning upwards from the sea. And this region, all along the island, faced towards the South and was sheltered from the Northern blasts. And the mountains which surrounded it were at that time celebrated as surpassing all that now exist in number, magnitude and beauty; for they had upon them many rich villages of country folk, and streams and lakes and meadows which furnished ample nutriment to all the animals both tame and wild, and timber of various sizes and descriptions, abundantly sufficient for the needs of all and every craft.

Now as a result of natural forces, together with the labours of many kings which extended over many ages, the condition of the plain was this. It was originally a quadrangle, rectilinear for the most part, and elongated; and what it lacked of this shape they made right by means of a trench dug round about it. Now, as regards the depth of this trench and its breadth and length, it seems incredible that it should be so large as the account states, considering that it was made by hand, and in addition to all the other operations, but none the less we must report what we heard; it was dug out to the depth of a plethrum and to a uniform breadth of a stade, and since it was dug round the whole plain its consequent length was 10,000 stades. It received the streams which came down from the mountains and after circling round the plain, and coming towards the city on this side and on that, it discharged them thereabouts into the sea. And on the inland side of the city channels were cut in straight lines, of about 100 feet in width, across the plain, and these discharged themselves into the trench on the seaward side, the distance between each being 100 stades. It was in this way that they conveyed to the city the timber from the mountains and transported also on boats the seasons' products, by cutting transverse passages from one channel to the next and also to the city. And they cropped the land twice a year, making use of the rains from Heaven in the winter, and the waters that issue from the earth in summer, by conducting the streams from the trenches.

As regards their man-power, it was ordained that each allotment should furnish one man as leader of all the men in the plain who were fit to bear arms; and the size of the allotment was about ten times ten stades, and the total number of all the allotments was 60,000; and the number of the men in the mountains and in the rest of the country was countless, according to the report, and according to their districts and villages they were all assigned to these allotments under their leaders. So it was ordained that each such leader should provide for war the sixth part of a war-chariot's equipment, so as to make up 10,000 chariots in all, together with two horses and mounted men; also a pair of horses without a car, and attached thereto a combatant with a small shield and for charioteer the rider who springs from horse to horse; and two hoplites; and archers and slingers two of each; and light-armed slingers and javelin-men, three of each; and four sailors towards the manning of twelve hundred ships. Such then were the military dispositions of the royal City; and those of the other nine varied in various ways, which it would take a long time to tell.

Of the magistracies and posts of honour the disposition, ever since the beginning, was this. Each of the ten kings ruled over the men and most of the laws in his own particular portion and throughout his own city, punishing and putting to death whomsoever he willed. But their authority over one another and their mutual relations were governed by the precepts of Poseidon, as handed down to them by the law and by the records inscribed by the first princes on a pillar of orichalcum, which was placed within the temple of Poseidon in the centre of the island; and thither they assembled every fifth year, and then alternately every sixth year—giving equal honour to both the even and the odd—and when thus assembled they took counsel about public affairs and inquired if any had in any way transgressed and gave judgement. And when they were about to give judgement they first gave pledges one to another of the following description. In the sacred precincts of Poseidon there were bulls at large; and the ten princes, being alone by themselves, after praying to the God that they might capture a victim well-pleasing unto him, hunted after the bulls with staves and nooses, but with no weapon of iron; and whatsoever bull they captured they led up to the pillar and cut its throat over the top of the pillar, raining down blood on the inscription. And inscribed upon the pillar, besides the laws, was an oath which invoked mighty curses upon them that disobeyed. When, then, they had done sacrifice according to their laws and were consecrating all the limbs of the bull, they mixed a bowl of wine and poured in on behalf of each one a gout of blood, and the rest they carried to the fire, when they had first purged the pillars round about. And after this they drew out from the bowl with golden ladles, and making libation over the fire swore to give judgement according to the laws upon the pillar and to punish whosoever had committed any previous transgression; and, moreover, that henceforth they would not transgress any of the writings willingly, nor govern nor submit to any governor's edict save in accordance with their father's laws. And when each of them had made this invocation both for himself and for his seed after him, he drank of the cup and offered it up as a gift in the temple of the God; and after spending the interval in supping and necessary business, when darkness came on and the sacrificial fire had died down, all the princes robed themselves in most beautiful sable vestments and sate on the ground beside the cinders of the sacramental victims throughout the night, extinguishing all the fire that was round about the sanctuary; and there they gave and received judgement, if any of them accused any of committing any transgression. And when they had given judgement, they wrote the judgements, when it was light, upon a golden tablet, and dedicated them together with their robes as memorials. And there were many other special laws concerning the peculiar rights of the several princes, whereof the most important were these; that they should never take up arms against one another, and that, should anyone attempt to overthrow in any city their royal house, they should all lend aid, taking counsel in common, like their forerunners, concerning their policy in war and other matters, while conceding the leadership to the royal branch of Atlas; and that the king had no authority to put to death any of his brother-princes save with the consent of more than half of the ten.

Such was the magnitude and character of the power which existed in those regions at that time; and this power the God set in array and brought against these regions of ours on some such pretext as the following, according to the story. For many generations, so long as the inherited nature of the God remained strong in them, they were submissive to the laws and kindly disposed to their divine kindred. For the intents of their hearts were true and in all ways noble, and they showed gentleness joined with wisdom in dealing with the changes and chances of life and in their dealings one with another. Consequently they thought scorn of everything save virtue and lightly esteemed their rich possessions, bearing with ease the burden, as it were, of the vast volume of their gold and other goods; and thus their wealth did not make them drunk with pride so that they lost control of themselves and went to ruin; rather, in their soberness of mind they clearly saw that all these good things are increased by general amity combined with virtue, whereas the eager pursuit and worship of these goods not only causes the goods themselves to diminish but makes virtue also to perish with them. As a result, then, of such reasoning and of the continuance of their divine nature all their wealth had grown to such a greatness as we previously described. But when the portion of divinity within them was now becoming faint and weak through being oftimes blended with a large measure of mortality, whereas the human temper was becoming dominant, then at length they lost their comeliness, through being unable to bear the burden of their possessions, and became ugly to look upon, in the eyes of him who has the gift of sight; for they had lost the fairest of their goods from the most precious of their parts; but in the eyes of those who have no gift of perceiving what is the truly happy life, it was then above all that they appeared to be superlatively fair

147

and blessed, filled as they were with lawless ambition and power. And Zeus, the God of gods, who reigns by Law, inasmuch as he has the gift of perceiving such things, marked how this righteous race was in evil plight, and desired to inflict punishment upon them, to the end that when chastised they might strike a truer note. Wherefore he assembled together all the gods into that abode which they honour most, standing as it does at the centre of all the Universe, and beholding all things that partake of generation; and when he had assembled them, he spake thus : . . . [Plato]

# BIBLIOGRAPHY

The author is grateful to the following authors and publishers whose works have inspired the writing of this book :

Abetti, G. and Hach, M., *Nebulae and Galaxies*, Faber & Faber, London

Allen, Richard H., *Star Lore, Their Names and Meanings*, Dover Publications, New York

Asimov, Isaac, *Eyes on the Universe*, Houghton Mifflin, Boston 1975

Bailey, James, *God-Kings and Titans*, St Martin's Press, New York

Berlitz, Charles, *The Mystery of Atlantis*, Avon Books, New York

Berlitz, Charles, *Mysteries From Forgotten Worlds*, Dell Publishing, New York

*The Bible:* Genesis, The Book of Revelation, Ezekiel

Bramwell, James, *Lost Atlantis*, New Castle Publishing, Hollywood

Burland, Cottie, Nicholson, Irene, and Osborne, Harold, *Mythologies of the Americas*, Hamlyn, London

Burridge, *Giants in the Earth*, Rosicrucian Digest, August 1965

Charles, R. H., *The Book of Enoch* (translation), Health Research, Nokelume Hill, California

Charroux, Robert, *The Gods Unknown*, Berkley Medallion, New York 1972

Clarke, Arthur C., *Report on Planet 3*, New American Library, New York

Clarke, Arthur C., *The City and the Stars*, New American Library, New York

Clarke, Arthur C., *The Exploration of Space*, Temple Press

Collyns, Robin, *Did Spacemen Colonize the Earth?* Pelham Books, London

Coon, Carleton S., *The Story of Man*, Alfred A. Knopf, New York

Von Däniken, Erich, *Chariots of the Gods?* Bantam Publishing, New York; Souvenir Press, London

149

# Bibliography

Von Däniken, Erich, *Return to the Stars*, Corgi Books, London

Donnelly, Ignatius, *Atlantis—The Antediluvian World*, Steiner Publications, New York 1971

Drake, Raymond W., *Gods and Spacemen of the Ancient West*, Sphere Books, London

Drake, Raymond W., *Gods and Spacemen of the Ancient East*, Sphere Books, London

Evans, J. D., *Malta*, Thames & Hudson, London

Getts, Charles, *The Circle—A Cosmic Symbol*, Rosicrucian Digest, February 1973

Hall, Manly P., *The Secret Teachings of all Ages*, Philosophical Research Society published by H. S. Crocker, San Francisco

Holiday, F. W., *Creatures From the Inner Sphere*, Popular Library, New York

Homer, *The Odyssey*, Dodd Mead, New York (translation by S. H. Butcher & A. Lang); Penguin Classics, Harmondsworth (translation by E. V. Rieu)

Homet, F., *Sons of the Sun*, Neville Spearman, London 1963

Honour, Allan, *Secrets of Minos*, McGraw-Hill, Toronto, Canada

Jackson, John G., *Man, God and Civilisation*, University Books, New York

Kolosimo, Peter, *Timeless Earth*, Bantam Books, New York

Lansburg, Allan & Sally, *In Search of Ancient Mysteries*, Bantam Books, New York 1974

Lewis, Ralph M., *The Mysteries of Egypt*, Rosicrucian Digest, December 1972

Luce, J. V., *End of Atlantis*, Thames & Hudson, London 1969

Mavor, James W., *Voyage to Atlantis*, G. P. Putnam's Sons; Souvenir Press, London

Merejkowski, Dmitri, *Atlantis Europe*, Steiner Publications, New York 1971

Pauwels, Louis and Bergier, Jacques, *The Morning of the Magicians*, Granada Publishing, England

Pickering, J. S., *1001 Questions Answered About Astronomy*, Dodd Mead, New York 1966

Plato, *The Critias*, The Loeb Classical Library, William Heinemann, London; Harvard University Press

Plato, *Timaeus*, Loeb Classical Library

Sendy, Jean, *Those Gods who Made Heaven and Earth*, Berkley Medallion Books, New York 1972

Spears, Stanley, *Universal Brotherhood*, Rosicrucian Digest, 1970

# Bibliography

Spence, Lewis, *Myths of Mexico and Peru*, George Harrup & Co., London

Sprague de Camp, L., *Lost Continents, The Atlantis Theme*, Ballantine Books, New York

Steiger, Brad, *Atlantis Rising*, Dell Publishing, New York 1973

Talor, Lord William, *The Mycenaeans*, Thames & Hudson, London

de Vaucouleurs, G., *The Discovery of the Universe*, Faber & Faber, London

Velikovsky, Immanuel, *Worlds in Collision*, Doubleday, New York

# INDEX

# Index

154

# Index

# Index

# Index

# Index

# Index

# Index